HARNESSING
GRIEF

A
Mother's
Quest
for
Meaning
and
Miracles

MARIA J. KEFALAS

BEACON PRESS
BOSTON

BEACON PRESS
Boston, Massachusetts
www.beacon.org

Beacon Press books
are published under the auspices of
the Unitarian Universalist Association of Congregations.

24 23 22 21   8 7 6 5 4 3 2 1

This book is printed on acid-free paper that meets the uncoated paper
ANSI/NISO specifications for permanence as revised in 1992.

Text design and composition by Kim Arney

Library of Congress Cataloging-in-Publication Data

Names: Kefalas, Maria J., author.
Title: Harnessing grief : a mother's quest for meaning and miracles /
   Maria J. Kefalas.
Description: Boston : Beacon Press, [2021] | Includes bibliographical
   references.
Identifiers: LCCN 2020010986 (print) | LCCN 2020010987 (ebook) |
   ISBN 9780807040256 (hardcover) | ISBN 9780807040263 (ebook)
Subjects: LCSH: Kefalas, Maria J., 1967- | Kefalas, Calliope Joy,
   2009—Health. | Metachromatic leukodystrophy—Patients—
   Pennsylvania—Philadelphia—Biography. | Metachromatic
   leukodystrophy—Patients—Family relationships—Pennsylvania—
   Philadelphia. | Parents of terminally ill children—Pennsylvania—
   Philadelphia—Biography.
Classification: LCC RC366.3.L48 K43 2021 (print) | LCC RC366.3.L48
   (ebook) | DDC 362.1968/30092 [B]—dc23
LC record available at https://lccn.loc.gov/2020010986
LC ebook record available at https://lccn.loc.gov/2020010987

For Pat,
the bravest man
I have ever known.

Contents

CHRISTMAS

It was Christmas morning 2009.

Just two days earlier, on December 23, I had given birth, at age forty-two, to a baby girl my husband, Pat, and I named Calliope Joy. Calliope is a family name; my sister and great-aunts and cousins were named Calliope. Students of Homer know Calliope is a daughter of Zeus, a goddess of epic poetry and song. Her divine power is to inspire beauty in the world. And Cal's middle name is Joy—the feeling that engulfed Pat and me when we first met our third child.

I don't know if I understood the perfection of that moment until years later, when our lives were transformed by such trauma and tragedy that we wondered how we would survive it all. We all have some perfect moments in our lives, and we usually miss them, or perhaps mark them down merely as a good day. But we are blind to the *perfection* until time passes; until we use time as a yardstick to measure and review this moment to realize the treasure it was. We can see perfection only from a distance.

That Christmas morning, there was snow on the ground, but the sky was clear and sunny. I sat in the lobby of the hospital with this new baby in my arms and my father seated next to me. My parents and Pat were so relieved. Despite the risks of having a child in my forties, Cal was perfect. Of my three children, she had been the easiest delivery, though she weighed more than eight pounds. Even though I was "advanced maternal age," Pat and I had not been inclined to terminate the pregnancy, but I had done the standard genetic screenings recommended by my obstetrician. All the testing revealed a healthy child.

Cal had been born in Pennsylvania Hospital, America's first hospital, founded by Benjamin Franklin. The rooms were stuffy and tiny, but the birth and delivery program was one of the best in the city, and if something went wrong Pat and I wanted the baby to have the best care. Her older sister, Camille, who was ten, and her brother PJ, who was five, had been born in the same hospital.

My dad and mom had driven down from their home in Massachusetts to see us and Cal, which meant missing Christmas with their other seven grandchildren, who still lived in my hometown of Lexington. Those grandchildren and other family members were disappointed not to have Papou and Yia-Yia (the Greek words for grandpa and grandma) there, but there was no way my parents would have missed out on meeting the new baby, checking in on me, and spoiling my older children. When they expressed concern about leaving the rest of the family behind, I chided them, "C'mon, how often do you get to see your tenth grandchild?"

There is an image I will always remember from that day. I was holding the baby, surrounded by flowers and gifts from the people who had visited us in the hospital. And my father kept trying to catch the eyes of passersby so he could brag about his granddaughter who was coming home on Christmas Day. "The best present anyone could ask for," he would say, beaming. He had always taken great pride in his children's accomplishments, but he was old-fashioned enough to believe that motherhood and marriage ranked higher than publications and promotions.

Having a baby on Christmas is a big deal. Even doctors and nurses are sentimental about the holiday. As the other poor souls headed to see loved ones on the oncology, ICU, or cardiac floors, I basked in the only good reason to be in a hospital on that day. As a student of Greek mythology, I should have realized I was tempting fate with my hubris, the sense that good fortune is earned, deserved, and secure.

It would take me years, after tragedy and grief and heartbreak struck over and over again, to realize that at this moment my life was the best it would ever be. Looking back, I saw no warnings that it was all about to collapse around us in two years. But maybe that's the point: when you get to this peak of happiness and joy, the laws of gravity instruct us, you must come down. The thing is, who wants to look down when you are headed up and the world seems to be nothing more than an expanse of uninterrupted bliss?

My pregnancy with Cal was unplanned, a total accident. As it turns out, after teenage girls, the second-largest group of women with unplanned pregnancies are forty-year-old women. I should have known better. After all, both my grandmothers had babies at forty-two. When my academic friends heard the news about my surprise pregnancy, they teased me endlessly because that same week I was scheduled to give a talk titled "Unplanned Parenthood." After the publication of my second book, on teen and single moms, the *New York Times* had dubbed me an expert on marriage and the family. The truth is, I didn't know anything truly profound about any of those things until Cal joined our family.

A month before Cal's second birthday, in December 2011, Pat made arrangements for a long-delayed vasectomy; we joked that there would be no more children with his second wife. When he went in to prepare for the procedure, he told the doctor about some back pain. Pat had been training to run a marathon. "Of course your back aches," I teased, "you have a toddler and you're in your forties trying to run a marathon." But Pat never had back pain. Because the doctor also noted Pat's sudden weight loss, he ordered a barrage of blood tests and scans. They revealed dangerously high levels of calcium in his blood, which means his bones weren't getting any. The radiologist's reports noted that Pat, who was forty-five, had the back of a man twice his age. The vasectomy would be forgotten, and Pat would be referred to an oncologist at Pennsylvania Hospital.

Pat would be seeing the doctor the Monday after Thanksgiving. That weekend I tried to tempt him with all his favorite foods, but his appetite had evaporated. The back pain was so pronounced he could hardly get out of bed; instead, he took his meals in an armchair in the living room because the wooden chairs in our dining room were now instruments of torture.

When we arrived at the hospital that Monday morning, it was clear I was the only one who hadn't realized Pat had cancer. The medical secretary did not look up from her desk as she handed me a brochure that read, "What to do when your loved one is diagnosed with cancer." I tried to give it back to her, but Pat silently motioned for me to put it in my bag.

We were ushered into an examination room, a place where doctors could have some privacy when they gave people bad news. There was only a small window looking out onto an alley. We were on the other side of the building from where Cal had been born. Pat would be seeing an oncologist named Lee Hartner. Dr. Hartner looks like a triathlete with his shaved head and athletic build, a look popular among oncologists. Perhaps the hairless look was offered as a proof of solidarity with their patients. Dr. Hartner moved efficiently and had a skilled poker face: a prerequisite for any good oncologist.

Dr. Hartner took the care to turn away from the computer to deliver the news; he looked Pat directly in the eyes as he spoke. I remember how he held Pat's gaze and did not blink, trying to make a connection with us. It was a trick I learned as a researcher, a way to ensure that the people you were speaking to knew you were focused on them and engaged. Years later we would learn that Dr. Hartner teaches medical students at the

University of Pennsylvania how to give patients difficult news. You could tell he understood that people would repeatedly relive the moment when they learned they had a cancer. It would even have a name: Diagnosis Day. Once someone learns they have a cancer, a clock starts ticking over their head.

"We think you have a disease called multiple myeloma," Dr. Hartner said in the same unremarkable tone a waiter would use to ask you if you wanted coffee with dessert. "Have you heard of it? It is a blood cancer." Pat nodded and absorbed the news silently. I shook my head and made a sound that sounded like a kicked dog. Dr. Hartner studied us both. Pat was the brave one or, at the very least, the stoic one. I was not.

"We need to admit you right now," Dr. Hartner said calmly, at the same time making an effort to emphasize urgency. Trying to keep me distracted, Dr. Hartner asked me if Pat's behavior had seemed strange or out of character recently. He explained that the two symptoms of hypercalcemia (high levels of calcium in the blood) are confusion and irrational behavior. This question offered a much-needed bit of comic relief. Pat could be rather obstreperous, but it was true that his behavior had become more extreme. He had defiantly insisted that our brand-new coffee machine was defective. He was convinced that the coffee tasted like it was tainted with metallic toxins. No one else could detect this contaminant, but Pat insisted, sending emails and making phone calls to the mystified customer service representative at Cuisinart. The company replaced the coffee maker with a new one that Pat immediately proclaimed had the same malfunction. He could not believe that *Consumer Reports* and the Better Business Bureau were not aware of the shockingly shoddy production of high-end coffee makers.

Before Pat could be transferred to the hospital, we would be sent to a room just one floor above the one where Cal had been born. Dr. Hartner asked if he could perform a biopsy on Pat's bone marrow. If Pat agreed, Dr. Hartner wanted to do the procedure right there in the examination room. Normally, it would be done with more planning and preparation and in a procedure room. But, Dr. Hartner explained, the sooner he could see how far the cancer had spread, the more quickly Pat could begin a treatment plan that was suited to the disease.

I was anxious about this but stayed silent. Pat agreed immediately.

As a graduate student at the University of Chicago, I had worked on a research project for a pediatric hematologist-oncologist, and I regularly had to describe a bone marrow biopsy to people. It requires using a large needle that is powerful enough to push through skin, muscle, and bone. Pat would lie flat on his stomach while the doctor placed this needle into his lower back and removed a small sample of bone marrow to test it to see if it was diseased.

Pat's back pain made it difficult for him to climb onto the examination table, which should have been our first indication that doing the procedure without anesthetic was ill advised. The moment Dr. Hartner inserted the needle, which seemed even larger than I remembered, blood spurted on Dr. Hartner and on the wall behind the examination table. Pat tried but failed to stifle a guttural wail of agony. He looked gray, and it appeared he was going into shock. Dr. Hartner was visibly shaken; the procedure had gone pear-shaped. It looked as if the young medical student who was shadowing Dr. Hartner that day might fold up like a lawn chair right there on the spot.

I didn't blame Dr. Hartner for what happened; Pat had been eager to find out if the cancer was in the bone marrow. But in the future, I would not hold my tongue with my concerns. Doctors operate with imperfect knowledge, and you must know when to speak up and ask questions or say, "That might be a bad idea."

What Dr. Hartner did not say as we waited to be admitted was that he believed the cancer to be stage IV and that 80 percent of Pat's bone marrow was diseased. The levels of calcium in Pat's blood were so high they were causing his kidneys to shut down, so he was in renal failure and was being considered for dialysis. What Dr. Hartner did tell us was that Pat was young and healthy and not suffering from underlying conditions such as diabetes or heart disease. He was optimistic Pat would respond to the double whammy of multiple blood transfusions to stop the damage to the renal system and chemotherapy to push the cancer back.

Having given birth to three children and having come from a family of doctors, I've never flinched at blood or medical procedures. I sat there in the corner of the examination room, never taking my eyes off Pat. Pat was my best friend, the father of my children, the only person who had ever made me feel beautiful and loved. He could not leave me. This was not how our story ended. When Dr. Hartner ordered medications for Pat to control the pain, and once the color started to return to Pat's face and Dr. Hartner and his medical student were steadier, I excused myself. No doubt everyone assumed that the blood and the screaming had left me uneasy. The truth was I had to flee because my emotions were making it difficult to take in air or sit and control my body. The terror was filling up my chest and lungs and mouth and ears. I kept telling myself I was not really going underwater so that I could still breathe.

"There has to be a social worker in an oncology practice where they give people bad news all day long," I thought to myself. The same coordinator who had wordlessly handed me the brochure pointed to where I could find the social worker, Carol Smith. Ms. Carol, which is how younger people address this respected elder African American woman, reminded me of the elementary school principals I had worked with in West Philadelphia. She greeted me at the door of her rabbit warren of an office wearing a conservative blue suit. Many of the buildings at the hospital are a century old, and space is a precious commodity. Ms. Carol's office barely had room for a desk and a chair, but a private office was just as valuable as a raise or a promotion. Without being invited in, I grabbed the small chair pushed up against the wall, ready to share my feelings and fears. I had assumed that is what a social worker did, help people like me process the bad news.

Ms. Carol was not unkind or insensitive. She dealt with cancer patients all day, and she worked at the practice for decades right up until her retirement a few years ago. But before I could say a word, she asked, "Are you the patient?" As soon as I answered no, Ms. Carol rose up from behind her desk and started to usher me out the door. She gently reminded me that everyone out there in that waiting room has cancer. The people who were sick were her and the doctors' and the nurses' priorities, not me.

Suddenly I was overcome with shame. I had wanted to lean on Pat for comfort. I wanted to hear him promise that he would live until his eighties and that the cancer would not steal him from me when he was so young. But I learned an important lesson that day. Even for those of us prone to cowardice and panic, bravery can be learned, or at least performed. There is no difference between being brave and acting brave. The other lesson from that day is that denial in managed, small doses has its uses. Pat was the one facing chemotherapy and biopsies and pain and fear over leaving behind his children and me. It was my job not to add to that burden.

That day established a division of labor for how we faced tragedy: Pat's stoic acceptance and my weepy, emotional meltdowns. He would keep me focused on doable tasks like talking to the doctors and handling the issues at hand, and it was my job to process emotions and be the shock absorber for feelings.

By dinnertime that Monday we would be settled into a hospital room, and this would become our second home for the next two weeks as Dr. Hartner worked frantically to save Pat's kidneys and get the myeloma counts moving in the right direction. In the oncology world we would quickly learn that multiple myeloma is a "better cancer," a close neighbor to the "good cancer" category. Plasma cells are stable, so the disease is not as fast-moving and aggressive as a blood cancer like leukemia, which attacks the white blood cells. But Pat's high tolerance for pain and disinclination to complain let the disease get dangerously out of control.

Pat was assigned a twenty-three-year-old nurse named Michelle, who had graduated the past June. We told her about twelve-year-old Camille, eight-year-old PJ, and the about-to-turn-two-year-old Cal. Her face grew more serious when she shared, "My mom was diagnosed with cancer when I was twelve years old . . . right here at this hospital." Before I could speak, the young nurse anticipated my question. "Yes, my mom is still alive; she is doing great. The best nurses work in oncology," the nurse explained. "I'm trying to work my way up to oncology by putting in my time here on the floor." As a parent, I didn't know what to make of the fact that this woman's reaction to the trauma of her mother's cancer diagnosis was to want to be an oncology nurse. Was this grit or a sign of some unresolved pain? Even though I was twenty years older than her, the young nurse seemed to sense that I needed guidance. "May I give you some advice?" she asked. I nodded. "You need to understand, once your parent is diagnosed with cancer you become an adult; your childhood ends." When a child learns how their parents are impotent against sickness and disease and tragedy, they can no longer be a child.

It horrified me that the gift my parents had provided me well into adulthood would be lost to my own children not long after they had stopped believing in Santa Claus and the Tooth Fairy. This was what people meant by childhood trauma. I had naively assumed that raising my children on the Main Line surrounded by beautiful homes and great schools would keep tragedy and suffering at bay. Now I could see the absurdity of such thinking.

In a day Pat was feeling better, and the doctors were happy with how his numbers were moving. Then Pat's sister called him from Ireland. We knew Pat's father, Paddy, had gone to Dublin to see doctors about pain and discomfort. Tests had shown a growth near his stomach. Because Paddy had long suffered from kidney stones and gallbladder issues, we hoped the growth was just part of those chronic gut ailments. But after surgery and a biopsy, the doctors found cancer. Pat was sitting in the hospital room getting his first chemotherapy infusion when he learned the news about his father. My mother-in-law was keening on the phone; she could hardly speak. It was pancreatic cancer.

Pat took in the news with the same silent resolution he had demonstrated less than twenty-four hours earlier when he heard his own cancer diagnosis. It was surreal. It seemed to me that the world was catching up on some sort of overdue notice. Life had been filled with too much good fortune and security, and the double-whammy cancer diagnoses struck me as fate's collection agency serving a repossession. In an act of bravery and self-preservation Pat did not explain to his family where he was or what was happening to him. He made me promise not to tell anyone either. Given my own tendencies for exhibitionism, my husband sensed that I wanted to post the news on Facebook and put our friends to work on a father-and-son cancer fundraising appeal.

My impulse was to scream at the top of my lungs, and Pat's was to turn inward to protect his parents and himself. His capacity to endure his suffering in silence was (and still is) beyond my comprehension. He tried to explain it to me once, saying, "It's easier to face it all silently since if I open that door, I'm afraid I'll lose all control." This is the difference between Pat and me. He believes emotions must be managed or contained or they'll engulf you. My feelings could be harnessed and used like a renewable energy source.

Pat's dad was in the early stages of dementia, and mercifully, on many days, my father-in-law appeared to forget he even had cancer. There would be no chemotherapy, just palliative care and hospice. Paddy had lived a full life, and the only things that scared him more than death were doctors and hospitals, so no one saw the point in a protracted battle against an enemy that had already won.

Much to my amazement, the lessons from Ms. Carol about not being a burden to Pat held firm. With difficulty, I attempted my own version of stoicism in the following weeks. I used every bit of strength I could muster to get up in the morning, take care of my children, and be a support to Pat. My efforts at suffering in silence were poor impersonations of Pat's Irish family and friends. Pat had left Ireland in 1992 to attend the University of Chicago, and we married in 1994. Over the years, when I spent time with Pat's relations, I was fascinated by how they shoved their feelings so deep down that they never saw the light of day. Death and tragedy were nearly celebrated among the members of Pat's family. As a boy, he had regularly accompanied Paddy to the Blessing of the Graves and to wakes where the body was laid out in the sitting room as the honored guest. After Frank McCourt's memoir *Angela's Ashes* was published, Pat's parents and aunts and uncles engaged in a heated discussion about how miserable their childhoods had been and how their stories of poverty and suffering could also have become an international bestseller and Hollywood film.

My parents—my father in particular—had sheltered me from his own family's suffering. Maybe it was because Dad had grown up in Nazi-occupied Greece and then lived through Greece's bloody civil war. Through a child's eyes, going to bed at night wondering if your neighbors might slit your mother's throat or rape her in her bed because her family were monarchists was not the stuff of song or poetry. For my father, death was something parents protected their children from—my parents took me to my first funeral at the age of sixteen. While Irish funerals are celebrations with music and drink and storytelling, Greek funerals are horrifying affairs with women wailing and people throwing themselves into coffins.

Pat and I are hardly alone in having fundamentally different understandings of grief and loss. When tragedy intrudes, even the most happily married couples don't collapse into each other's arms and experience anguish and grief under a single flag.

This only happens on the Hallmark Channel.

Two months later we faced another blow when the blood in my father's urine appeared to be caused by bladder cancer, and a biopsy confirmed that it was stage III.

In those weeks after Pat's diagnosis, I had come to rely on my father most of all. For an hour on the phone for a few days a week, I could break character and be who I really was: the weepy, freaked-out mess who could only think about how Pat's illness affected me. Just as he had all my life, Dad told me I would be okay and that I could handle this. No one propped me up better than Dad could. He even teased me about how Pat was a walking and talking cliché, like John Wayne in *The Quiet Man*. He would remind me that Pat would not change now, even in our time of need. After all, we revert to our true selves in a crisis. As much as Pat and I were different, Dad would say, there was no question Pat adored me and that he was worth the effort. In the aftermath of Dad's cancer diagnosis, I lost the person who was helping me be brave. I was now on my own. Even I could not be so selfish as to ask Dad to take care of me now that he was sick too.

Knowing my father was vulnerable, realizing that he could not protect me anymore, left me unmoored in middle age. Yet my own children had not finished middle school when they learned their parents were powerless to keep them safe from the world's suffering. We never needed to tell Camille about her father's diagnosis. With the help of Dr. Google (and a classmate who had been diagnosed with lymphoma), she had puzzled out the symptoms on her own. So, when I offered Camille a child's definition of multiple myeloma—as a disease in Daddy's blood—Camille responded, "Is it lymphoma or leukemia?" At twelve she had proven herself a skilled diagnostician and far more willing to face the truth of her father's symptoms than I was.

PJ was just seven when his father was diagnosed. I raced to talk to PJ before Camille (whom Pat and I nicknamed "third parent" for her impulse to mother her brother and sister) showed him a TED Talk on cancer research. PJ knew that both of his grandfathers had cancer, and he knew that such a diagnosis caused death. I decided not to use the word "cancer" in my introductory discussions of his father's illness. Camille could understand the different forms of cancer, but a seven-year-old would have no way to distinguish between chronic cancer and a terminal diagnosis. When I broke the news about why Pat was in the hospital and sick, I explained that Daddy had a disease in his blood. PJ accepted this explanation without comment. Then, after PJ wanted to know if his father would get better, I answered, "They are giving Daddy medicine to feel better. The disease is still in his blood and it is not going to go away, but he won't feel so sick." PJ was young enough to still trust what I was saying to him. If Mommy could say, "Daddy would feel better soon," that seemed to satisfy him.

We all celebrated when the first rounds of treatment shrunk my dad's tumor by a third. For a month I believed that both my dad and Pat might keep their cancers at bay for years. You did not have to be cured of cancer, my father would say; "you just need to keep it from moving." Besides, he would add, "the doctors don't really want to cure it or else they would put themselves out of business."

My father started treatment at Massachusetts General Hospital after his biopsy results were in. Its infusion center was a monument to the promise of new cancer treatments. My dad became well known to the regulars at Mass General's Yawkey Center because he would hand out icons of the Virgin Mary and flirt with the nurses. He would share the holy oil he carried around with him in his pocket and promise other patients that if they prayed hard enough, miracles would seek them out. I was busy taking care of Pat and the kids, and while I could not make the trip to Boston, my sisters and my mom would update me. Whatever worries nagged at my father, he kept them from intruding on our weekly phone calls. He took care to call on the day he got his steroids so he could sound strong and energized. Even though Dad was sick, he never let me give up hope. "Pat will be fine, you will be fine, and the kids will be fine," he would repeat over and over on the phone. I realized later that he never promised that he would beat his cancer.

Dad's reassurances gave me hope. So, too, did the fact that, though Pat had been diagnosed with cancer, multiple myeloma was not like a glioblastoma. Upon hearing that Pat had multiple myeloma, the counseling psychologist working with newly diagnosed patients offhandedly said, "Multiple myeloma . . . that's a good one." You had to guess he had been helping people prepare to tell their husbands, wives, and children some truly bad news, so, in this context, Pat's cancer was not exactly good news but not the worst you might get from an oncologist. He explained that he had not intended "to diminish the seriousness of the situation," and I assured him that the slip of the tongue was the most reassuring thing that had transpired in a week. If a guy who spent his days speaking with cancer patients was not panicked, and even seemed nonplussed, I would try to follow his lead.

One of my best friends and colleagues, Susan, who had been among the first people I called the day Pat was admitted, had been treated for lymphoma as a teenager and then for early-stage breast cancer when she turned forty. Susan is amazing in a crisis and was one of the few people who hardly flinched when she heard Pat, my dad, and father-in-law all had cancer. Of all our friends she was one of the few who could make herself useful in a hospital. Living with cancer all her life had resulted in an absurdist sensibility. Yes, Susan agreed, multiple myeloma "isn't a bad one." She noted wryly, "Penn's multiple myeloma support group is gigantic. All these guys keep showing up for the free coffee, so they must not be dying in significant numbers."

My younger sister Cathy started researching everything she could about multiple myeloma, contacting physicians at Mass General and Boston's Dana-Farber Cancer Institute. The Boston branch of my family had long believed that Harvard was the only place your doctors should earn their medical degrees. My mother and sister wondered if we should relocate to Boston because the University of Pennsylvania might not have people clever enough to care for Pat.

After learning about the early promise of something called CAR T-cell treatment, Dr. Hartner told Pat that if he could hold on for another five years, multiple myeloma would be a very different disease. This would become my mantra; whenever people asked about Pat's health, I would just repeat the same phase: "Pat's cancer is a better cancer, moving into the good cancer category." I would list the new breakthroughs and drugs and the promise of biologics and immunotherapies. I sounded like a marketing campaign for Big Pharma, but there was no time for, or point in, dwelling on the bad outcomes. My sister Cathy kept sending me blogs about multiple myeloma patients running marathons and climbing Mount Kilimanjaro.

My father's nearly pathological belief in miracles was like a warm blanket when we spoke on the phone. "Don't worry about nothing," he'd say. "Pat is too stubborn for cancer to stop him." He would laugh: "You need to have hope."

DIAGNOSIS

When people asked me how Pat and I were doing, and I shared with them that my husband, father, and father-in-law all had cancer, I would go on to say that I found the multibillion-dollar cancer-industrial complex oddly reassuring. When you go to the Abramson Cancer Center at the University of Pennsylvania, the similarities between a drive-through McDonald's and infusion are hard to ignore. Infusion centers and even bone-marrow-transplant floors are orderly, efficient places. There's far less crying and terror than you might imagine. People quietly and patiently stand in line, stream Netflix, or take a nap.

As a kid growing up in the 1970s and 1980s, my view of cancer was based on the film *Love Story*. Patients lay in hospital wards with buckets for vomiting under their beds, slowly (and picturesquely) fading away. By the time Pat was diagnosed, the treatments that would take hours and make you puke your guts out had been replaced by daily pills and shots and acupuncture suites, meditation gardens, sandwich carts, and gift bags. One of Pat's oncology nurses confided to me once that you need to worry only when the nurses start to look worried. And in all the years of Pat's life with cancer, there has been little panic except for the botched biopsy in Dr. Hartner's office.

Just as we were coming to terms with Pat's chronic cancer, signs that things with Cal were not quite right started to add up. The first came while she was eating her lunch one day. She was sitting in her high chair when, out of nowhere, her body vibrated like an electric current was passing through her. It was over in a few seconds. The incident alarmed her babysitter so much that the girl cried out in fright. I ran from the kitchen to the dining room to see what was wrong. The babysitter said, "I have never seen a baby do that!" I quickly reassured her, saying, "Babies do all sorts of strange things."

Though I said nothing to Pat or the babysitter, I was alarmed enough to do some Google searches for tremors and seizure activity. My quick research turned up no clues. As the mother of two older, healthy children, at first it was easy to talk myself off the ledge when it came to Cal. Camille and PJ were above-average students and athletes, and there was nothing in our family history to suggest any genetic disease. And in a bit of irrational thinking, I had come to believe Pat's, my father's, and my father-in-law's cancer diagnoses meant we had filled our quota of misfortune and sickness. Pat would later point out that a social scientist trained in statistics should have understood that tragedy is not rationed out according to an actuarial table.

Cal's most glaring issue was her speech. At age two, she reliably said only a few words: ball, Daddy, elephant, PJ, Camille, and dog. Dog and ball were clear, but PJ sounded more like "Jay" and Camille was "Mille." Dogs fascinated her and balls were the toys she played with, mostly with her doting big brother. Cal's bond with PJ was unsurprising. My son had been the only person enthusiastic about the pregnancy from the start. He had lobbied Pat and me for months to have a little brother. Upon hearing about Cal's arrival, PJ was overjoyed, and he even reminded us of the excuse we had offered for not wanting another baby: "I thought you said you were too old."

Cal's lack of words most assuredly troubled Pat and me, but there were plenty of convenient explanations. There was the fact that Cal's nanny, Palloma, was from Brazil and English was her second language. There were Cal's chronic ear infections and the resulting surgery to insert tubes. PJ had been slow to speak but had proven himself to be a gifted student. As a busy working mother, I thought I must have been to blame for Cal's lack of speech. Work, and Pat's and our dads' cancers, kept me so distracted that I didn't spend enough time with Cal. I didn't read or play with her as much as I had with the older children.

At Cal's next doctor's visit, our pediatrician noted that she had fewer words than most children her age, but she declared Cal to be hitting all her other milestones. The doctor said Cal seemed to be thriving and that she saw nothing to raise alarms. Cal's appetite was fine; in fact, she could stuff her face with meatballs. It was true that she seemed a bit clingier than my older children, but that was easy to explain away. Pat and I indulged her. We were now older parents, less inclined to set limits and say no.

The pediatrician initially did not seem alarmed, but we asked her to refer us to Montgomery County's early intervention team. They would conduct a thorough assessment of Cal, and the earliest they could see us was February 2012.

At her peak, Cal used around twenty words. I would read ten books a day to her and the words just didn't stick. Cal could dribble a soccer ball better than a three-year-old, but she didn't like the structure of school. My sister Cathy joked that Cal would never be "easy." Classrooms in a Montessori school, where Cal attended preschool, are earnest and quiet, but Cal would run around the room yelling and laughing hysterically. The only thing she did right during class was eat her snack and clap along to the good-bye song. And she was the only child in the class who could manage to open the heavy door.

It is accurate to say Cal ruined every class. The perfect Main Line moms in white cashmere and Louis Vuitton were so annoyed with Cal, who thwarted their efforts to micromanage their toddlers' achievements. The other children in the class would sing and play dress-up, while Cal seemed out of sync and mystified about why we were there. After Cal pushed another little girl out of her way while the pair played with a dollhouse, the girl's mother pulled her daughter away. "Leave Cal alone, she needs to be by herself."

Cal never said "Mommy," but she said "Daddy." Surprisingly, it doesn't bother me that she never said "Mommy"— none of my children did. I like to think "Mommy" was just so obvious and self-evident that there was no need to give me a name. Though the point is debated in family lore, Cal's first word may have been the Portuguese word for shit (*merda*); no doubt it was a word Palloma used a bit too often around Cal. Cal's only sentence was "Are you alright?" This was also from our nanny, who would ask that question of Cal when she shoved food into her mouth too quickly or tripped. Cal would mash all the words together so it sounded like she was saying "awyouawright." When she saw me cry, she would ask, "Are you alright?" Cal may have struggled to speak and play with her peers, but her sense of empathy was fully formed. "Are you alright?" was one of the last things she would say to me.

The night before the county caseworkers were scheduled to arrive to assess Cal, we cleaned the house from top to bottom. They would come to evaluate Cal's speech, behavior, and overall progress, but we believed they were also assessing us. The idea was that early intervention could help Cal catch up and become prepared to attend school. Pat and I wore our work clothes for the meeting, making the point to introduce ourselves as professors so the team understood we were peers and colleagues. Somehow it felt important to convey that we were caring, educated, well-off parents with two older healthy children.

Three women arrived for the evaluation. The supervisor, who could not have been older than thirty, made a point of introducing herself as the person in charge. One of the women was absolutely silent throughout, save for whispering the occasional questions to her colleagues. She was in training, her "supervisor" explained. The third woman was the most outgoing and cheerful; she told us she was the team's "child whisperer." It was her job to get children to play and interact. The supervisor explained that three strangers coming to a home and playing with a toddler was unlikely to elicit a typical reaction ideal for a baseline assessment.

Things got off to a bad start immediately. When the supervisor explained to Pat and me about how there are seven senses, Pat nodded politely, but I needed to ask, "Don't you mean five senses?" Pat kicked me. Then, when the supervisor started to explain that "social behaviors need to be learned and taught to children," Pat pinched me. Nobody wanted to hear me lecture about Jean Piaget's theory of cognitive development in children.

There were the expected questions about Cal's hearing and ability to maintain eye contact. She had had a hearing assessment a few months earlier and the test had found nothing out of the ordinary. As for the question about eye contact, Cal and I would do staring contests in the bathtub for hours. When I wondered what might happen if Cal showed no interest in playing, the cheerful and most bubbly of the women pulled out a bag of brand-new toys. She promised Pat and me that she had never seen a child who did not want to leap into her arms by the end of the session. It didn't take long for Cal to demonstrate how misplaced this confidence was.

Each woman took a turn with Cal, and every single one of them might as well have been a boulder. When they asked Cal to pick out a toy or identify a color, she stared at the toy motionless for a moment and then turned away. When asked to stack blocks, she shoved one in her mouth. The truth was that Cal did not play with toys so much as observe others playing with them in front of her. For most of the session, despite all the appealing toys and books scattered around the living room, she stayed in the corner playing in the cardboard boxes that PJ had turned into a playhouse for her.

Though they insisted they were not testing Cal, we all knew this was a kindhearted lie; of course they were. And at each test Cal was not officially being given, she failed spectacularly. Much to Pat's horror, I played "the cancer card," working into the conversation the cancer diagnoses of Pat, my father, and my father-in-law. The team looked troubled at the news of the cancer trifecta and seemed to accept all these "reasons" for Cal falling behind. We were not like the other families; we had a compelling explanation for why Cal was struggling. It seemed plausible that she was getting lost in the shuffle of a family facing a series of health crises.

The visit dragged on for hours. What was supposed to be an evaluation of Cal's speech had now become an assessment of her physical therapy, occupational therapy, and socialization issues. Cal was advanced physically, but she did not interact well socially with other children besides her siblings. When other children played instruments in music class and could follow two- or three-step directions, Cal would sit there staring. Pat and I would tell people that Cal "has her own way of doing things" and "has some sensory issues." All these clues did not point to anything genetic, much less fatal. Cal was the kid you tried to make excuses for, and I had become the mom excluded from the play group and pitied because something was just a little off. To my face, the other moms tried to be kind and offer platitudes about how "each kid progresses at their own pace."

A few weeks after the meeting, the evaluation team created a special education plan for Cal, set out in a twenty-page Individualized Education Program, or IEP. Every county in the US provides such services for free for pre-school-age children. But the resources in an affluent area like Montgomery County were particularly strong. In Philadelphia, a kid like Cal would have been lucky to get one therapist assigned to her case. But because of where we live (and given how poorly she had fared),

Cal's IEP was exhaustive. An army of therapists came to work with Cal on her speech, social behavior, and motor and physical development three days each week. To accommodate all the therapists, we turned the living room into a classroom with toys and books and equipment to help with Cal's low muscle tone and fine-motor skills.

My mom, a retired schoolteacher, cheered on this educational boot camp. There was no doubt in my mind that I could help compensate for Cal's delays; they were just another problem to be fixed. I had succeeded at everything I attempted; Cal would be no different. For a time, she seemed to improve. With all the people working with her day in and day out, our home was transformed into a private nursery school with Cal as its only pupil. Playing was no longer a whimsical pursuit; it was a military campaign. It seemed as if I was spending less time in the office and devoting more time to Cal. Each morning before she worked with the therapists, we would read so many books that my voice would become hoarse. Cal and I played together for hours, took long walks, and read and played with blocks and puzzles and charts with colors. When she performed a task or uttered a word, I took note of the event to show the therapists. How I grasped on to these faint signals of progress. Looking back, none of it was working, but I refused to believe that Cal would never catch up.

The IEP team's report made me question many of the choices I had made for Cal. When she had a seizure caused by a sudden high fever (a so-called febrile seizure) a few months before the IEP meeting, I should have refused to leave the hospital until a neurologist evaluated her and ordered an MRI to get to the bottom of what was wrong. Febrile seizures are common in toddlers, and the ER doctors did not think to ask for more testing. Looking back on this time, a part of me can't help but think that a more protective mother, a better mother, would have listened to her gut and been brave enough to recognize the mounting evidence that something was terribly amiss.

At the playground, as children younger than Cal spoke in complete sentences and climbed the slide and the jungle gym, she would stand frozen, uncertain of her next step, carefully navigating the uneven ground or the ladder to get onto the equipment. When mothers asked how old Cal was, I lied. Subtracting a few months off her age helped me save face and protected us from the well-meaning moms who measured their children against others to establish how gifted and precocious they were. It was strange to be the mother on the wrong end of the comparison.

There was a little girl at our church, also named Calliope, who was just a few months younger than Cal. One day during the coffee hour after services I watched the two girls side by side. There was no denying how much Cal had fallen behind. The other Calliope talked and played with her older sisters and could do complex tasks. Unlike Cal, who could not sit still and hated to be strapped into her stroller, the other Calliope quietly held her sisters' hands, read books, and ran and jumped effortlessly. That day it seemed to me that Cal would not be like my other children. But I would not fully understand what this meant for another few weeks.

In May, three months after the evaluation, Cal's occupational therapist asked to expand the team to bring in a physical therapist because Cal, in her estimation, was not only not improving but was deteriorating. It was as if Cal was afraid of her own body. Then one day Pat yelled for me to come see something. Cal suddenly could not climb steps anymore. She was falling. My mother noted with alarm that Cal was walking on her tiptoes, the way a toddler just learning to walk might. She was no longer simply delayed; she was now losing milestones. Regression is a big, waving red flag. When a child starts losing the ability to walk or speak, it is, without exception, a sign that something is terribly wrong. Years later, a world-renowned neurologist would say to me that he always tells medical students, "Remember this adage: if a kid is regressing, get them some testing." Yet Pat and I proposed the theory that maybe Cal's hearing issues had impacted her balance. It was an extraordinarily naive explanation, but Cal's recurrent ear infections led us to get an appointment with the most respected otolaryngologist in the region. We were determined to see one of the best doctors at Children's Hospital of Philadelphia (CHOP), even if it meant we would not get an appointment until late June.

Pat was at chemo, so I took Cal to the hospital. As the doctor watched Cal try to walk across the room, he seemed to recoil. Unlike Dr. Hartner, who looked you straight in the eye and was so present as he gave you bad news, this doctor clearly wanted to run out of the room. He turned away and started typing notes in his computer. His only words were, "If I were you, I would bring her to a pediatric neurologist right away. This has nothing to do with her ears."

I left the office holding Cal and crying. I was hyperventilating, and the nurse offered to call my husband or someone to come pick us up and drive us home. My first thought was that it was a brain tumor. Another version of the cancer that was tearing through our family. It must be cancer. The nurse gave me a child-size Dixie cup of water, and I reached out for another one. She offered a kind but delusional hypothesis: "Maybe your daughter's gait issues are a reaction to everything that is going on around her." I clung to this ludicrous notion long enough to manage the drive home.

On the road I was able to contact Cal's regular pediatrician. She told me to bring Cal in at 8:00 on Saturday and reassuringly said that we'd figure it out. So that's what I told Pat that night. He wanted to cancel the kids' soccer game he was coaching and come with us to see the doctor, but I dissuaded him, especially as he adored being with the kids and watching them play. "There's no reason for us both to spend the day in the hospital," I said. "I'll let you know if anything comes up." Was I being brave? Or just fighting off the reality of how serious it all was?

Cal and I were the only people at the office on the weekend before the Fourth of July. Most other families were gearing up for summer vacation and dropping kids off at camp. Cal's doctor made her walk back and forth in the examination room, and it was like she was seeing Cal for the first time. All she said was, "You need to go to CHOP right now."

It was a gorgeous Saturday morning in June and Pat was enjoying a much-needed reprieve from doctors, hospitals, and chemo. For some reason I tried to protect him from what the doctors were telling me. The idea of being around Pat and our older children made me seasick. This was really bad, and the last thing I wanted to do was let them see how afraid I was. The singular lesson I had learned from my parents was to protect your children at all costs. If that meant lying to them or hiding from them, that was far better than revealing the ugly truth that the suffering of the world can find children and that parents are powerless to stop this from happening.

I bundled up Cal on that perfect summer day and raced to CHOP, which is just seven miles from our home. On the drive into the city I watched the mothers pushing strollers and walking their dogs along the Schuylkill River. I despised these women for their healthy children. I called Pat to say only that Cal's doctors wanted her to get a full workup of blood tests and even an MRI since we needed "to rule out something serious." I insisted he finish the game and said that we'd meet later. This was a time for me to use that newly honed skill of suppressing my emotions. I needed to leave out just how alarmed the doctors were over Cal's condition. Now that Cal was in trouble, I thought I should protect Pat, so I worked to keep him out of the hospital. For some misguided reason, I thought I could take care of Cal on my own.

Then I called Sharon, one of the therapists who had been working with Cal. I asked her to meet us at the hospital so she could describe to the doctors what she had been seeing in her sessions with Cal. We called Sharon the drill sergeant because she pushed Cal the hardest, but she was also the first person to press us to see that Cal was not improving and actually regressing. A few days earlier I had asked her to come observe Cal in her Gymboree class. She could see that Cal could not manage to play with the balls or use the equipment; she was now crawling when she would have walked before. "Callie wants to be with the other children," Sharon said. "I would be more concerned if she didn't want to be near the other children." When I started to cry, Sharon hugged me and tried to comfort me. "Don't worry, Mom, we will help her, I promise."

We headed straight into the emergency room, where one neurologist after another came in to ask us the same questions. They were muttering terms like ataxia, hypotonia, hyperreflexivity, and low muscle tone. The doctors hardly looked at me because they were studying Cal so intently. Every single one asked to see her walk, and they all hit her on the knee with those odd little hammers.

The doctors wanted to know if Cal had seizures. Months later we would learn that the tremors and the staring sessions could have been related to seizures. At the time we did not know if Cal had ever had a full-blown seizure, but there was now growing evidence of seizure-like activity. An MRI was being ordered, but because it was the end of June, all the new residents had just arrived, so things were a bit crazy, and on the weekend before the Fourth of July the hospital was also understaffed.

Cal was given an IV, and the nurses drew blood for a series of tests. The bloodwork kept coming up negative for anything viral. The more manageable explanations for Cal's symptoms were being eliminated at a dizzying pace. What I didn't realize at the time was that they were prepping her to go under anesthesia for emergency surgery in case they found something such as a brain tumor. Since Cal was not being allowed to eat or drink, I had to distract her with movies and books and songs.

As they moved us up to her room on the neurology floor Cal started to sing. I had spent the past several months working with therapists and teachers to get her to sing, and suddenly, as we rolled her gurney up to her hospital room, she started to sing "Itsy-Bitsy Spider." The words were barely decipherable, but there was melody and sounds closely approximating language. I had sung those verses so many times, during her bath, while she ate breakfast, at the play group, and when she played with her toys. She had never before sung along, not even humming. But now, as the doctors and nurses walked her to her room, as she was hooked up to monitors, she was singing. Sharon could not believe it. It would be the last time we would hear Cal sing.

My friend Susan also came to my side that afternoon. She had been out on a bike trip with her husband and her two girls but left them behind to be with me in the hospital, still in her biking clothes. Susan and Sharon remained with me at the hospital until Pat could get the older kids settled at home and arrange for the nanny to watch them. What had begun as a visit to the doctor was escalating in urgency.

My texts and voicemails to Pat had been brief and vague. I didn't want to lie to him, but I saw no point in offering details until there was something definitive to say. The past six months of chemotherapy, his hospitalization for renal failure, and his father's failing health made me protective of him. Keeping him out of the hospital for a few more hours was both futile and an act of compassion. Pat arrived at the hospital around dinnertime and paced the room, fidgeted with his phone, and studied Cal for signs of what might be wrong. By this time Cal had been admitted for evaluation and was hooked up to monitors and an IV.

I called my sister's sister-in-law, Elayna, a neurologist in New York City, and she coached me on how to work with the residents and get the best help for Cal. She walked me through the diagnostic flow chart they would use. The best-case scenario, she explained, was that they would order a brain MRI. She told me to push the doctors to include the spine in the

MRI. The standard protocol was to have a brain MRI and then have a spinal MRI only if the brain MRI revealed nothing. She explained that doing both tests at once would help get us answers faster. At one point I got on my hands and knees in the emergency room to beg the doctors to get Cal the test. My pleading worked, and the two MRIs were authorized. Elayna's advice was so good that one of the doctors wondered if I was a doctor too.

I kept telling the doctors and nurses it could not be cancer because my husband, father, and father-in-law all had been diagnosed with that disease in the past few months. And I started praying to God, "Please don't let it be cancer." I kept hoping for Lyme disease, but when that test came back negative I retreated and prayed for lupus and then MS. When you start hoping for epilepsy or a mini stroke, you know you are in trouble.

The slogan on all of CHOP's billboards, "Where hope lives," seemed to mock me as our hope slipped away with each passing hour. This is the hospital C. Everett Koop led back in the 1970s, where he and his colleagues pioneered the field of pediatric surgery. The hospital's multimillion-dollar branding celebrates breakthroughs and miracles. And yet these neurologists were far from confident. There is a joke about neurology: neurologists have two diagnoses. The first is "We do not know what it is and there's nothing we can do." The second is "We know what it is, and there's nothing we can do."

The first inkling that there was a diagnosis worse than a brain tumor came when a nurse explained to me that the MRI was used to find genetic metabolic disorders that attack the brain and central nervous system. "They are quite rare," she explained, "but they are serious." She went on, whispering in hushed tones since I am pretty sure our conversation violated some HIPAA privacy rule. "I have only seen one in my six years as a nurse. That little girl had come all the way from Russia, I think, and when the parents got the diagnosis, there was nothing to be done. The family just went home, and I never saw that girl ever again. . . ." The nurse's voice started to trail off. It was clear the little girl had died soon afterward.

The MRI was scheduled for Sunday night. A resident came in to say that the bloodwork had revealed nothing, so Pat and I approached the MRI with a mixture of relief and anxiety. We knew the doctors hoped to find nothing, but if there was something to find, we would see it on the MRI. If there was something wrong, this was one of the best children's hospitals in the world. We would face whatever we had to.

After cold and flu season ends in the spring, the number of patients in the hospital goes down, so even though Cal's room could accommodate two patients, we had it to ourselves. Cal slept in a crib right in the center of the room. At night, the nurses would bring in clean sheets, towels, and toiletries. In the 1990s, the old hospital buildings with large communal wards had been remodeled with private rooms and couches that became beds so parents could sleep every night with their children.

On the far side of the room was a wall of floor-to-ceiling windows with a panoramic view of the city and the Schuylkill River that a CEO would have envied. The hospital's generous donors made sure that sick children and their families were treated as honored guests. Whenever we had been at CHOP before, the stunning views and bright colors had been reassuring. But now a place that tried to look so cheerful seemed like false advertising.

Over the next twenty-four hours the distinction between the clothes I slept in and wore in public blurred. When I caught my reflection in the mirror, I hardly recognized myself. There was no color in my face save for the black circles under my eyes, and my hair was filled with tangles. I have never been vain, but even I was startled by what the past few days had done to me. Most of the other mothers in the hospital looked the way I did. The more experienced mothers—the frequent fliers—who had spent months or years in and out of hospitals with their children, sensed that they had an initiate in their ranks. They knew better than to reach out and welcome me. I was still in the death rattle of denial, fighting the mounting body of evidence that Cal was not okay.

The radiology techs came to escort Cal to the MRI. She would be sedated for the procedure so they let us come with them so we could keep an eye on her. The walk seemed to take forever. The MRI room is in another section of the hospital, and CHOP is actually a collection of several different buildings, so we zigzagged through the service corridors and elevators to the basement of the hospital. It was strange to be there in the middle of the night; usually the place would have dozens of patients going in and out for tests, but we were the only ones there. The two techs caring for Cal asked us about the meaning of Cal's name and wondered about our family, as we all pretended that a two-year-old getting an MRI on a Sunday night was nothing out of the ordinary.

We then had to make our way back to Cal's room on our own. Had Pat not been with me, I would have gotten lost wandering the hospital corridors. The MRI would take an hour, so Pat waited in Cal's room. I lied and told Pat I was going to the cafeteria, but I went to the tiny chapel on the hospital's first floor instead.

By ten o'clock Cal was back in the room. A radiology tech, a different one from the two we had met earlier, told us that "the test revealed nothing emergent." It was an odd, formal, legalistic way of speaking. The young man looked ashen, sort of like a flight attendant assuring passengers to stay calm as the oxygen masks popped out of the overhead cabin. Pat turned to me: "That sounds okay, right?" "It means that they don't need to take her into surgery, yes. That is good," I said, lying to him and myself.

The tech's news had come with an unsettling asterisk—"A doctor would be coming to speak to us in the morning"—suggesting that they had indeed found something. And when I revisit this moment, I realize that the young man knew it was bad, but he was relieved that it was above his pay grade to talk to the parents. Another mother and father might have forced him to tell us what he had seen, but, for once, I let things be. The past six months with doctors had taught us that there is no rush to hear bad news.

Pat and I argued about who would spend the night in the hospital. I won. Pat is a terrible sleeper, and he would not have gotten any rest at all. I could sleep anywhere. Even though no one would imagine it was going to be easy, to me, staying in the hospital alone with my thoughts was much better than going home and having to be okay in front of Camille and PJ. Pat had the harder job, it seemed to me, to leave Cal and deal with Camille's and PJ's questions and fears.

After Pat left the hospital to go home, I returned to the chapel again. Pat liked to joke he was a "collapsed" Catholic, and I didn't want to hear one of his speeches about the Church's sex-abuse scandal. I just wanted to light a candle for my little girl. In that final prayer, before our lives changed forever, I asked for something different. I asked God to help me accept whatever the doctors found. Then I got greedy, threatening God: "I will never forgive you if it is cancer. This will be our final conversation if you give my little girl a brain tumor." In the end I would never forgive God for giving me just what I asked for.

That prayer was the first, tiny step in the multiyear transformation that would burn away the person I was and replace it with someone nearly unrecognizable.

On Monday morning Cal was still sleeping and I was just waking up when the doctor walked in. She was an attending, and there was a younger woman by her side. This woman's name tag read "social work."

Doctors, especially attendings, don't need a wingman when they tell you your kid has Lyme disease or even epilepsy. But a social worker and a doctor were coming to see us first thing on a Monday morning; this was the worst sort of news and I knew it. For some reason I glanced at the clock: 7:48 a.m. When the Khmer Rouge came to power in Cambodia, Pol Pot restarted the calendar at zero to mark the end of the old epoch and the start of a new one. This was the same thing, the very moment when our old life came to an end and our new life started.

Cal was just starting to wake up, and I took her out of her crib so I could hold her on my lap. I think I imagined she could be a shield between the doctor and me.

The conversation with the doctor was astonishingly short. There was no "I am sorry" or "We have some news." The doctor said, "We believe your daughter has a disease called leukodystrophy. We suspect it is a form of the disease called metachromatic leukodystrophy."

I knew enough Greek to understand that leukodystrophy, which seemed to be a combination of leukemia and muscular dystrophy, must be awful. So my next question was blunt: "Is Cal going to die?"

And then the doctor answered, "Yes, it is fatal, and we have no treatment or cure."

I held on to Cal and started weeping. Not delicate tears or even loud sobs. It was this convulsive sort of crying that makes you wretch. It turns out vomiting and peeing in your pants are not uncommon reactions in these sorts of situations. Cal seemed to think my crying was amusing, so she giggled and smiled. From the start, she was better at this than any of us.

Getting really bad news from doctors is nothing like it is on TV shows or in the movies. There is no reassuring presence, much less a handsome one with George Clooney's chiseled features and brown eyes flecked with specks of gold, seeking to reassure you with words of wisdom or a tender embrace. Doctors are trained in how to give bad news in medical school. They are like fighter pilots: they go in at top speed, drop the bomb, and get the hell out of there. You really can't blame them; telling a parent their kid has a death sentence is like throwing a pile of raw meat at a caged, rabid bear. Doctors understand they can't linger or else they'll get mauled. They are also smart enough to know there is nothing they can say to make it better. They might let their guard down and get sloppy. You see, when they start to feel human, they will be tempted to say those little lines that seem like they should help but really don't, things like "Miracles happen every day" or "It will be okay" or "I am a parent too and I know how you feel."

The other thing I have learned about doctors is that they spend most of their careers avoiding the most fundamental truth of their profession: children die. Places like Children's Hospital of Philadelphia build their brand on miracles. The social worker who had come in with the doctor to make sure they got out in one piece tried to console me, but I shoved her away. She sensed my grief was going to a dark and dangerous place. There were other patients to see, after all, and I would not be the only parent getting bad news that morning. The social worker did offer me a single piece of advice that has stuck with me all this time: "Try to learn to cry in the shower to keep it from your husband and children."

Pat was home with the children, and so I phoned him. Suddenly my voice was gone, and all I could do was croak like a frog. It felt like I was choking but somehow I could still breathe—a condition called *globus hystericus*. Pat knew it was me on the phone, but he could only make out animal sounds. Pat was yelling into the phone, "Maria, what's wrong! Tell me what's happening!" I handed the phone to the doctor to make her tell Pat herself. I remember thinking, "You're the doctor, that's your job to give him this news. I cannot bear to destroy him with this." It is something that shames me to this day, that I could not tell Pat about Cal. Pat is the bravest person I know, and he never would have done that to me.

Pat appeared at the hospital fifteen minutes after I called, and he made the doctor tell him the news again. The trip normally takes forty minutes; he must have driven on the highway at ninety miles per hour to be at the hospital so soon. We had nothing to say to each other. I was mute and he was trying to get his questions answered without disturbing me. After the doctor left the room I took four Valium, chased down with a kids'-size apple juice from the hospital's nourishment room. Floating away for a while seemed like a highly reasonable strategy.

When I awoke from the Valium-induced coma, I called my parents, my priest, the therapist who was working with Cal as part of her early intervention team, the provost of my university, my sister's sister-in-law the neurologist, Cal's pediatrician—anyone in my phone. I would say the same thing over and over again: "Hello, it's Maria, we are at the hospital, they just told us Callie is dying." Needless to say, that's quite a conversation killer. No one had anything to say to me—priests, professors, or doctors. Even the clinical psychologist who had been working with me for a few months, who had been helping me cope with my dad, husband, and father-in-law having cancer, was left speechless. He said, "Oh shit, I've got nothing." It was astounding how bad everyone was at offering words of comfort. Years later, I would learn that in a moment of great need most people make the mistake of thinking that there is something perfect to say that will make things better. The truth is there is nothing to be said, and all you can do is show up. And be present.

Pat called no one; he stood off in the corner, pacing back and forth, occasionally speaking to the doctors, Googling leukodystrophy on his phone.

Now when I speak to families experiencing what we did that day, I advise them to pay attention to the people who run to your side. These are the ones who will come to your aid time and time again. You will be surprised by who that is. They might not be your best friends or your closest family members, but they are the bravest. Many of them will know firsthand the pain you are experiencing. They will be the people who know what it is like to sleep in a hospital room and have your life torn apart by a doctor's news or a 3 a.m. phone call. They might be there just to hold your hair back when you vomit into the toilet or to make sure you don't walk around the hospital in your bare feet. They are the first responders who run toward the most terrifying thing. The bystanders want to save themselves and flee in the opposite direction. The people who rushed to the hospital that morning included Susan, my friend who had met me at the ER on the Saturday when Cal was admitted; Laurie, a professor at Rutgers with Pat; and our oldest friend in Philadelphia, Julie, our son PJ's godmother. These were the people we knew would be able to help us now in our time of need.

The room was mostly silent except for Cal's occasional laughter and the *Shrek* DVD that had been on a continuous loop. I had curled up into a ball on the couch, trying to hold myself together and pretending to sleep. Everyone was being thoughtful and whispering around me, but I could hear them. When I heard Pat and my dad and my father-in-law had cancer, that had been frightening, overwhelming. This was something else completely. Hearing that Cal was going to die was an act of violence. It felt like I was coming apart on a molecular level. It felt like I was dying too.

Cal was discharged the day the doctors informed us she was going to die. We did not want to be in the hospital any longer. We felt abandoned and betrayed by the promise of science and medicine at the world-famous hospital surrounded by the billboards with the slogan "Where hope lives." The social worker returned to the room one last time before Cal got discharged, and she told me that one of her colleagues would be working with us to enroll Cal in Medicaid. "The doctor will also fast-track Make-A-Wish," she said. It was astounding that all they could offer Cal was welfare and Make-A-Wish.

MERMAID

Many nights, the mermaid, she stood by the open window, look-
ing up through the dark blue water, and watching the fish as they
splashed about with their fins and tails. She could see the moon
and stars shining faintly; but through the water they looked
larger than they do to our eyes. When something like a black
cloud passed between her and them, she knew that it was either
a whale swimming over her head, or a ship full of human beings,
who never imagined that a pretty little mermaid was standing
beneath them, holding out her white hands towards the keel of
their ship.

—HANS CHRISTIAN ANDERSEN, *The Little Mermaid*

Before we left the hospital Pat tried to speak to the neurologist, but she was so weary from the morning's drama that she advised him to research the disease for himself. An internet search would reveal what a horror show MLD is: imagine ALS and Alzheimer's disease having a monstrous offspring, and that will give you an idea of MLD.

A child with MLD appears healthy at birth, but by the age of two the brain's white matter (or myelin) starts to disintegrate because the child has a mutation on the ARSA gene that makes it impossible to produce an enzyme called arylsulfatase A. This enzyme is crucial for the brain and central nervous system's healthy development. Now we had an explanation for why Cal, whom we'd nicknamed Happy Feet because she was always in motion, could be losing the capacity to control her body. Suddenly her inability to play the drum in music class or color a picture in preschool made sense. One neurologist told us that by the time a child begins to show symptoms, the disease is a wildfire burning out of control. The terrified tech who brought Cal back to the room that Sunday night would have seen the damage to the brain. Anyone could have. A healthy child's MRI is all grays and blacks, but the MRI of a child with MLD would have glowing white everywhere showing where the myelin was dying.

Children with MLD who can speak say the disease makes it impossible for them to move their legs, control their bladders, or say the words they have in their heads. The damage to the central nervous system causes severe neuropathy, making it feel like their body is on fire from the inside. The disease also causes outbursts of anger and creates difficulty with concentration. Cal's trouble interacting with peers might have had a genetic cause.

Over the next few months, the online chat forums and Facebook pages I frequented predicted that Cal would lose every milestone—the ability to walk, talk, and feed herself—in a matter of months. She would be paralyzed within the year. In the disease's final stages, typically by the age of five, patients become blind, experience dementia, and become nonresponsive, eventually falling into a vegetative state. Years later, when I would meet newly diagnosed leukodystrophy patients' families, they would say that this disease makes them envy parents whose kids have brain tumors. I could not disagree.

Every human being has two copies of about thirty thousand genes, one copy inherited from their mother, the other from their father. Our genes tell our cells which proteins to make. Each protein is a tiny machine, and every cell in our bodies is built out of millions of these little machines working together. Proteins break down food, transport energy, and keep our cells healthy. Cal had inherited two faulty versions of the ARSA gene, and MLD was the result. Pat and I each have a broken

ARSA gene and a working one. The working copy prevented us from getting sick. But with two defective copies of the gene, Cal's body couldn't produce the single enzyme known as aryl-sulfatase A, and this was killing her.

Although geneticists believe one in one hundred people is a carrier of the ARSA mutation that causes the disease, the probability of two carriers having a child who inherited two copies of the mutation was smaller than getting struck by lightning. But when it happens, waste cannot be recycled, and fats known as sulfatides accumulate in cells. An abundance of sulfatides in cells that make myelin, the substance that insulates and protects nerves, causes progressive destruction of tissue throughout the brain, spinal cord, and other parts of the nervous system. All these years later it is hard for Pat and me to accept that just as Cal had inherited my curly hair and brown eyes and Pat's swanlike neck and stubbornness, we had also given her the genes that were killing her.

Many people have heard of cystic fibrosis, sickle cell anemia, and spinal muscular atrophy. What they have in common with MLD is that they are monogenic, caused by one broken gene. Among the thousands of monogenic disorders, lysosomal storage disorders and leukodystrophies represent a particularly terrifying subgroup. Before advancements in genetic testing and MRI technology, MLD and the other leukodystrophies were categorized under the umbrella of mysterious "wasting diseases" that would run through families and strike down children.

Individual types of leukodystrophies are quite rare; some forms of these diseases may impact just a few hundred patients on the planet. Although doctors cannot be certain, since the disease is commonly misdiagnosed as cerebral palsy, MLD is thought to be one of the more common forms of leukodystrophy. Experts guess the disease impacts between one in forty thousand and one in one hundred thousand births. But the numbers are still small. Around the world just 3,600 babies are born with MLD every year.

While MLD impacts just a few thousand children in the world, when you add all the leukodystrophies and related diseases together, they affect one in five thousand births, making them more common than ALS and as common as cystic fibrosis. We would learn later that Tay-Sachs disease, Canavan disease, and adrenoleukodystrophy (ALD) are all leukodystrophies. (ALD, the so-called Lorenzo's Oil disease, was the subject of the 1992 film by that name starring Susan Sarandon and Nick Nolte.) In the years since Cal's diagnosis, I have sat on panels for the National Institutes of Health and addressed the Food and Drug Administration about her disease, but back then I refused to learn the name of it or say it out loud.

It was difficult for me to tell people when they asked what was "wrong" with Cal. There was simply no delicate way to talk about how the kid who had once run now seemed afraid of her own body. In those early days I liked to pass for the parent of a healthy child. Pat and I joked about how when people noticed something was wrong or heard Cal was ill, they would cock their head and ask, "How are you doing?" or "How is your daughter?" Pat and I would come to call this "pity chitchat."

Sometimes they would offer their own experiences with a family member who had been diagnosed with Down syndrome or cerebral palsy, as if a special-needs child were the same as a dying one. It was hard not to yell and scream, but in these moments we tried to impersonate sane, reasonable people when confronted with these well-meaning but idiotic questions. The worst thing was the toxic positivity of people declaring that "doctors are wrong all the time" or "your daughter will get better and beat this." Or when people compared our tragedy to the time they thought their child had lupus.

Answering people's questions and explaining Cal's diagnosis to my elderly parents and colleagues at work made me relive the worst twenty minutes of my life all over again. No one had heard of MLD, and the idea that the finest doctors in the world had no treatment to offer went against everything people assumed about medicine. There were no videos or guides to help us or refer our friends to. "Couldn't the people at St. Jude's Hospital for Children help?" "What about Shriners?" Or "Doesn't Jerry Lewis still do those telethons?" No. Cal did not have cancer or cerebral palsy or muscular dystrophy. There was nothing to offer her.

I tried out several ways to tell people what was wrong with Cal. In the beginning, I would tell them Cal had a disease in the same family as the Lorenzo's Oil disease. In the 1980s, Lorenzo Odone's parents, Michaela and Augusto, embarked on a desperate search to find a treatment for their son to clear out the long-chain fatty acids that were accumulating in his body and damaging his brain and central nervous system because of adrenoleukodystrophy.

Lorenzo's father, an economist with the World Bank, disrupted the staid world of research medicine by teaching himself about neurology and biochemistry in order to find a treatment for the disease. He called out the medical establishment for abandoning rare diseases because developing treatments for them brings neither fame nor fortune. The Odones were truly remarkable patient advocates, inspiring a generation of families to believe that they could play a critical role in driving research.

ALD and MLD are in the same family, but it became problematic to draw the comparison, as people kept wondering why Cal was not getting the oil that was supposed to cure her. The truth of Lorenzo's Oil and ALD was far more nuanced than the Hollywood version—and Nick Nolte's Italian accent.

Lorenzo's Oil is real; many ALD patients use it. However, it is no cure. Some research suggests it might have some benefit in slowing down the onset of the disease, but the oil cannot reverse damage to the brain or central nervous system and is useless once the disease becomes active. And whatever benefits it may or may not provide are limited to children with a different form of leukodystrophy than the one Cal had. A different gene was causing her body to produce insufficient amounts of a different enzyme. It soon became easier just to say that Cal had leukodystrophy, a disease in the same family as Canavan and Tay-Sachs. In the predominantly Jewish Main Line, everyone knew about Canavan and Tay-Sachs. It was a pretty efficient way of getting the curious strangers out of my face.

Nothing shut down a conversation quicker than telling a stranger your kid was dying. I recognized the power of whipping out Cal's diagnosis and I made no effort to soften the blow by using euphemisms such as "medically complex" and "special needs." Cal's diagnosis was destroying our lives, and weaponizing Cal's tragedy to unsettle the clueless people with healthy children made me feel more in control.

In the weeks and months after the diagnosis I could not sleep. Insomnia was a completely new experience for me. My sister Cathy, who had always been an insomniac, told me it made things worse to try to force myself to sleep. She advised taking walks. It was summer, so I would take strolls through the neighborhood late at night, wearing my pajamas and flip-flops, no bra, and my curly hair wild. I had become a ghost haunting my old life as a Main Line soccer mom. The houses in our neighborhood are old—more than a few were built a century ago—and they are set back from the streets. With their air conditioners running during the summer, no one noticed me on my evening strolls. Secretly I hoped someone would come out to see why I was outside crying; no one ever did. I would imagine all my neighbors at home sleeping, safe in the knowledge that their children, who could run and play and go to school, were sleeping as well. I despised my neighbors for the good fortune of having healthy children and healthy husbands.

After we came home from the hospital, a nun I had left a message for in the chapel named Sister Alice called to check in. Sister Alice had worked at CHOP for thirty years. Her time there had made her a compassionate witness to all manner of suffering and had left her with hope and a faith in miracles.

This astounded me. Was Sister a fool or just deluded? How could she have seen hundreds of children die and still believe in God? Even if we did not agree about God and faith and miracles, she understood that the only comfort she could offer was to be a witness to my grief. The only advice she offered was to be skeptical about the doctors' predictions for Cal. "No one knows what the future holds," she insisted. "Miracles happen every day."

If Sister had not been a nun I would have screamed at her and asked her to leave me alone. This hope seemed cruel. Cal was dying. There was nothing left to say or do. What I could not understand back then was that Sister Alice's notion of miracles was much bigger than saving Cal. For me, a miracle was a cure for Cal, but what Sister Alice knew was that miracles take many forms. They are not always what we imagine or hope for, but they are always possible.[1]

The next week became a blur of follow-up tests and evaluations before we met the new neurologist who would be overseeing Cal's care. Cal would have to be fitted for braces and a wheelchair and have her swallowing evaluated for the risk of choking. There were discussions about the need for a feeding tube. At the occupational therapy clinic, the therapist handed me a notebook the size of an Oxford English Dictionary in which to carry Cal's medical records and the results of her MRIs and other tests.

At one of our doctor's visits a social worker popped her head in to see how "we are all doing." For this "we," she meant Pat and me. Despite my uninterest in talking, the social worker pulled up a chair and pushed in close to speak to us. "So what do you think about at two in the morning?" I suspected this was a tried-and-true question for parents like us, allowing her to evaluate how likely we were to be feeling suicidal or depressed. Pat lied and said he slept soundly. I did not want to lie, but I did not want to reveal how bad it was because sharing the whole truth might get me placed on suicide watch. So I shared what I believed to be an amusing description about my unfolding nervous breakdown: "To be honest, I think about how we are screwed. We are so totally fucked." The social worker looked concerned. People don't curse at the Children's Hospital of Philadelphia. I tried to laugh, and then the social worker's grin got bigger—not because she thought I was witty but because she did not have any other response. "You don't understand," I continued. "I actually made a list of how you know you are totally screwed. Do you want to see it? It's like the lists David Letterman would do on his show." Deciding that I must be some variation of okay, the social worker promised to get me her email. We never saw her again. There is a lot of turnover among the social workers in the neurology program at CHOP. It's a pretty brutal job dealing with parents like us for fifty thousand dollars per year.

As soon as the social worker left, Pat chided me. "Why do you even talk to them?" he hissed. "Don't you understand they are just doing their job to check in on us? They don't *really* want to know how you are feeling." This had never occurred to me. I assumed they truly wanted to listen to me, and that they might have some insights on how to help. But Pat just shook his head and said we were on our own. I did not believe that, but sometimes it was easier to say nothing.

I started writing a journal for myself. The list would be among the first entries. "Pat, I still think my list is funny, it just needs the right audience," I said. Pat sighed. "I don't think that's how humor works. Either it's funny or it's not."

TOP TEN REASONS YOU KNOW YOU ARE SCREWED
1. The doctors can't look at you and/or they break down in tears right before your eyes.
2. The nurses tell you that they can't stop thinking about you and that you are in their prayers.
3. The people on the phone at your insurance company tell you they are worried about how you are holding up.

4. All your friends, even the cheapest and the most broke ones, never let you pick up a check anymore.
5. You wish it was a brain tumor.
6. Your shrink tells you, "I've got nothing."
7. The people at Make-A-Wish promise to fast-track your family's dream vacation.
8. A Catholic priest says, "Job had nothing on you."
9. You don't care if you eat, shower, do your laundry, go out, change your clothes, buy new clothes, wear makeup or a bra, or deal with unwanted body hair ever again.
10. You can now relate to being one of the little old ladies who spend all their time at Starbucks wearing a sweater on an 80-degree day with makeup that makes them look like Bette Davis in *What Ever Happened to Baby Jane?*

I spoke again with my sister's sister-in-law, Elayna, the New York–based neurologist. Her research had not identified any promising clinical MLD trials or miracles lurking in the wings. She confirmed what Pat and I had learned: the only possible treatment option was a bone marrow transplant, a risky procedure that—under the best circumstances—might slow the disease's progression for a time. The same procedure had a 30-to-60-percent chance of killing Cal faster than the disease. Further, Cal was not a good candidate, as bone marrow transplants had been most successful in patients who presented with symptoms after the age of four. Elayna told me, "The only thing I can say is that when you look back on this time in the years to come, you need to say you didn't have any regrets."

Father Chris, our priest from St. Luke Orthodox Church, is one of the people we spoke to in the days after Cal's diagnosis who knew how to conduct himself around parents like Pat and me. One day he appeared in our kitchen and demanded to know what he could do to help. When Pat and I lied and said we were fine, he refused to believe us. "That's not true, tell me what you need." At that point we were finding it difficult to bathe Cal. She would scream in the tub because she was having trouble sitting up on her own and when I picked her up, she would scream because she was afraid she would fall. "We need to remodel the bathroom," I said. Father listened and took some notes. "Now was that so difficult? To tell me how we can help," he said. By the end of the week he had spoken to a member of the church who would pay our contractor to remodel the bathroom with a walk-in shower. Our benefactor never contacted us—we never even had the name of the person to thank.

Father Chris's wife, Michelle, showed up next.[2] She pulled out a piece of paper to take an order of our favorite foods. Pat's chemotherapy had left him with a lackluster appetite, and PJ was a picky eater, so I said, "We don't want to put people out." Michelle persisted, saying that the aunties and grandmas of the church would take turns cooking for us, and a cooler would be dropped off at the front door. Having grown up with my father's aunts, I knew that the white-haired widows of the church who dressed only in black existed to provide their services for funerals and miscellaneous tragedies. There was no problem that a roasted chicken, a pot of lentils, or a tray of baklava and Greek Easter cookies called *koulourakia* could not fix. Greeks have a saying: "The beans saved Greece." During World War II the German occupiers did not like beans, so when food was in short supply the Greeks managed to survive on the beans the Germans turned up their noses at. This was the motto of the army of widows. Fearing a freezer filled with food that would go to waste, I tried to explain. "The ladies of the church are so kind, but they really don't need to do this. Pat and I are going to be fine. We all like pizza," I lied. Michelle grabbed my hand and looked me straight in the eyes and said, "You really don't seem to understand. This is happening."

For months afterward, the cooler on our front porch was filled every day with loaves of home-baked bread, spinach pie prepared with hand-rolled pastry dough, spaghetti and meatballs, and cakes. Tupperware containers were waiting for us when we got home and our house soon was overrun with containers of every description, large and small, with purple, red, blue, and white lids. Most were filled with food lovingly prepared by kind people so eager to do something to help in those terrible days. The food might be a carefully cooked cherished family favorite, or it might be a Costco rotisserie chicken. You never knew. PJ and Camille would peek into the containers warily to see if there was something they might be tempted to eat.

Some containers were filled with meals prepared by neighbors, friends, and colleagues, but many more were assembled by complete strangers who thoughtfully called to find out what foods the children ate. Camille: everything. PJ: nothing. Cal was on a special diet of yogurt smoothies because of her troubles swallowing and chewing.

It didn't take long for me to become furious about the containers that were filling every free bit of space, even in my china cabinet. One day I had a tantrum when no one was home and I threw them at the wall and on the floor, cursing them as if they were the cause and not just a symptom of our current circumstances. I yelled, "I wish they could go back to where they came from!" The Tupperware was a symbol of community and compassion but also a daily reminder that I couldn't take care of my family.

Some nights, if I didn't take walks to deal with my insomnia, I would sit at the dining room table filled with despair, eating the food that had been dropped off at our door. I ate compulsively, hoping it would fill up my sadness and make me feel less afraid. One night I ate a pork loin like it was a giant Tootsie Roll of meat.

Twelve-year-old Camille was horrified and suggested that I needed to develop a healthier relationship with food. "Mom, don't be offended, but maybe you should try to be more like me.

I feel like I am the healthiest person in this house when it comes to what I eat." With my daughter staring at me as I shoved food into my mouth and with as much patience as I could muster, I said, "My darling, if I am hungry I will eat a giant piece of meat. I'm sorry you don't like it, but I want to eat it."

Those first days home I felt like I was dying, and years later, I would realize that I was. The person I once was, the person who looked forward to sending her daughter to kindergarten or teaching her to swim in the ocean, ceased to exist. A mother's dreams for the future are inextricably linked to her sense of self, and human beings who have nothing to look forward to become zombies stumbling through life and missing the defining feature of their humanity: hope.

When we got home from the hospital I did not want to be around Pat and my older children because I didn't know how to shield them from my anguish. The only thing that made sense to me, the only thing that kept me alive, was holding Cal for hours. We would watch movies and read books and go to the pool. For a very long time it seemed to me that I needed to be with her every waking hour because the doctors had told us we had just three years.

I was convinced that a good mother could never leave Cal's side. It was a sin to spend time with friends or selfish to go to the gym or work on a new book because she needed me. Years later I would learn that what I felt was something called anticipatory grief. In extreme cases, parents who have been told their child is dying stop going to work or bathing or eating because all they can do is stand watch and wait for the child to die.

Anticipatory grief is grief in three time zones simultaneously: your past, your present, and your future. For me this meant mourning the way Cal had been, so all the artifacts of her old life, her toys and shoes and the photos of how she used to be, were sources of agony. I had asked Pat to take down all the photos of her when she was a baby. It was Camille who asked me to give away Cal's toys to our beloved preschool because the sight of them brought her such heartache. All of us, especially PJ and Camille, struggled—and still struggle—with how to mourn our old life before Daddy and Cal got sick.

In the present we needed to accept that we were now a family with a medically complex child with a life-limiting illness. Our life of music lessons and soccer practice and school had to make room for hospice nurses and doctors and medical equipment and hospital beds. We now lived in a constant state of alert, wondering if this was the day we would need an ambulance to take us to the emergency room.

And the future was no longer about anticipating graduations and birthdays and summer vacations to Cape Cod. All of us understood that a terrifying inevitability was heading toward us and there was nothing any of us could do to change it.

The pool gave me the most comfort. Each day, as soon as we could get Cal fed and dressed, we would go there. In the water, the Cal from before her diagnosis returned. I am sure the neurologists, with all their jargon about how enzyme deficiency damages the sheath of the myelin, could explain why water helped her brain to function better than it could on the land. They might say it had to do with the way the water helped her body process the messages her brain was sending. But I preferred to see it as proof that Cal was a magical creature. It was during aqua therapy that a young occupational therapist named Kristy Pucci nicknamed Cal the Mermaid.

Indeed, it was comforting to think of Cal being transformed into a beautiful creature rather than dwelling on the medical explanations for a degenerative disease. In my grief I came to believe that Cal was not like other children because she was the Mermaid, too special and rare and pure to live among humans. And in the water her essence came through.

Whenever Cal and I were in the water in the days and weeks after she was diagnosed, in these trancelike moments I would pray. It was not a prayer to God but rather the expression of a feeling that would engulf me when I was in the water with her. Just staying in the water with my Mermaid was my idea of perfection, my heaven.

In the water my prayer was this phrase over and over again, a whispered song: "Mommy loves her Cal. Mommy loves her Cal." I would say that dozens of time each day. Then I would say, "Mommy knows you are not going to stay for long, but try to hold on for as long as you can and let me know when Mommy has to let you go." In these perfect moments with Cal, I would try to be careful in my words with her. How I longed to say, "Mommy will make it better" and "Mommy isn't going to leave," but these things were not true. The Mermaid seemed to understand that better than I could. But in the water it was impossible to hide the truth with sweet, false words. Mommy could not make it better and, far too soon, our Cal would be gone.

What I describe as prayer can be more accurately described as unfettered access to my love for Cal. My love for her was otherworldly and divine, and yet I never prayed to God after he had answered my prayers in the hospital chapel asking that he not give Cal cancer. My relationship with God is complex. I see God in the perfection of my daughter. I understand, with all my heart, how God's love is not possible without suffering. And humanity requires suffering, grief, and pain to experience joy and love, and to find wisdom and purpose. Yet my rage at God comes from the simple fact that losing Cal is too high a price to pay. Those days right after Cal was diagnosed I was already able to see the paradox of how suffering would make me a better human being. The rage over losing my Mermaid made me gag and choke, but even then the truth of this was clear to me.

The bathing suit I wore in the pool was ripped and faded. It was astounding how grief had given me more than a passing resemblance to the gruesome sea witch from *The Little Mermaid*. The realization made me laugh. Grief had transformed me into this numinous creature. Like my Mermaid, it seemed I lived with the humans but was no longer one of them. When I watched parents ignore their perfect children who could walk and play, or when I overheard a parent become impatient with a child for falling down, I pitied the humans for the tiny way they lived. Each day that passed it was harder to remember how I could ever have been like them. I wondered how they could not go to the sea and ache with joy at the sight of the beautiful and healthy children.

That summer I would have visions or dreams; I couldn't be sure if I was awake or not when these images came to me. Cal would be floating in some sort of blue netherworld—it could have been the sky or the sea. There would be a light in the distance and Cal's curly hair would be floating above her in waves. She would never speak, but she would gaze at me, never sad, never frightened, never happy; this was a place where such emotions did not exist. And there would be shimmering light reflecting around her. I would try to speak but no words would come out. There was no need for words in this place.

It was not heaven, but it was the place in my dreams that felt divine and supernatural. Even if Cal was still living among the humans, this was the place where my Mermaid actually dwelled. Cal could not mourn the life I expected her to have, and she lived in a place that humans could not understand. She was the Mermaid watching all of us, fascinated and curious, longing to be a part of this world but separated—misunderstood, silent, and coming to life only in the water, unable to live among the rest of us.

THE PORTRAIT

The neurology division's administrative assistant called to confirm our appointment to return to the hospital on the fifth of July to meet one of the two doctors at CHOP who treated children like Cal: Dr. Amy Waldman. Regular patients wait months to see a specialist like Dr. Waldman. For Cal, Dr. Waldman would be coming in early just to meet with us; we would be her first patient that Monday after the holiday.

Her photograph and biography on the hospital's website weren't very reassuring—Dr. Waldman was fifteen years my junior. Trained at Johns Hopkins, the Thomas Jefferson University School of Medicine, and then CHOP, she had only just finished her fellowship. "Impressive credentials, without question, but she is so young," I said to Pat. "Why would anyone so young want to take on a disease so horrible?" Pat listened to me but offered no response.

The nurses who were managing our case and who were not too terrified to speak to me (after all, I had threatened to murder the next neurologist by using their own reflex hammer against them) assured me that Dr. Waldman "is one of the good ones." All I knew was that July fifth hung over my head like an executioner's axe. There was no point in returning to the scene of the crime, to learn in excruciating detail how we would lose Cal. She was going to die; what would be the point of spending another day at the hospital to hear from another doctor that there was nothing they could do to help.

I was drowning—I had actually called my primary-care physician to ask which symptoms would require in-patient treatment for a mental collapse. She asked the question every doctor asked me: "So are you going to harm yourself?" I responded, "No." "But," I said, "it feels like I am dying." "I know," the doctor answered. What I had assumed to be an alarming symptom, she viewed as normal and totally expected given the circumstances. "You are much better off at home than in the hospital, trust me," the doctor said. But in the beginning I could not understand how doctors could just let me go home and suffer like this on my own. Much later I realized they had been right. There was no point in delaying facing up to the reality of our new lives. There was no treatment or therapy that could change what was happening to Cal and the rest of us.

It didn't help that my birthday falls on July 2, which meant that it was now associated with Cal's diagnosis. Even as a kid I had always wished for a different birth date. No one was around; the Fourth of July was the sort of popular holiday when people left to spend time with family. The only way to make sure anyone came to a party was to have it on the last day of school in June. Now, celebrating anything seemed pointless and absurd, but I told myself that having a party with our friends would be a distraction, perhaps offering some relief from the debilitating grief.

What do you give the mother of a terminally ill kid? When our friends asked about presents, I joked about wanting nice jewelry. Instead, one of our friends set up a fund in Cal's honor at CHOP. It raised ten thousand dollars in a few days. People also brought booze, someone gave us a tree to grow in our backyard, and another friend gave me a spa package. In spite of everyone's best efforts and the thoughtful gifts, there was an unavoidable sadness about the day, and years later a friend who was there joked that my birthday party had been so dreadful that he wondered if he would ever attend another one again. With nothing to celebrate, the party was merely a wake for the happy, comfortable existence that we had once enjoyed.

~

P at bought me a pendant with an angel from a well-known New York designer that was supposed to signify courage. The piece was stunning, and I wore it every day for months. The only piece of jewelry I own that means more to me is my wedding ring. I had never placed much stock in angels; the way they were portrayed in Hollywood movies and television shows seemed silly. But this one was inspired by Michelangelo and was supposed to bring peace. And more than anything else, peace is what I craved.

Pat's angel reminded me of the Victorian-era practice of creating pieces of art to remember a deceased loved one or making jewelry out of a dead child's hair. Before photographs, and at a time when the death of children was far more common, mourning jewelry was a way to remember lost loved ones. At the party, a colleague of mine from the art department suggested making a piece of jewelry or a portrait in honor of Cal.

The latter idea appealed to me immediately.

It was Queen Victoria who had popularized mourning jewelry in the wake of her own epic grief over the death of her husband, Prince Albert, when he was forty-two. My mother had a rose-gold ring with dark hair braided into the metal that had belonged to her grandmother. To me, as a little girl, it was macabre and magical. The dark-brown hair was so intricately woven it appeared to be a design carved into stone or maybe an embroidered fabric. My mother explained that my great-grandmother had made the ring after the death of one of her daughters. My grandmother lost children too: a baby named Arthur, who died at eighteen months, and a nineteen-year-old daughter named Elaine. The grief for all the children who had been lost seemed to have been imprinted on the ring. My mother wore it often when she thought of her mother or of the miscarriages that you were not supposed to talk about back in the 1960s and 1970s. With the ring, grief was handed down through generations like an heirloom. A child who died became a story or a spirit that the surviving siblings brought with them as they moved through their own lives.

Long before I realized how much I would share in common with my great-grandmother and grandmother, the story of the ring seemed like something out of the fairy tales I spent so much time reading as a girl. But now that I faced the kind of grief the women in my family had experienced, the idea of mourning jewelry seemed completely logical and the idea of creating something beautiful out of such loss became irresistible. But since mourning jewelry is no longer in fashion, I could find no way to commission such a piece on Etsy. So I settled on a painting, a far more socially acceptable option. The painting could capture Cal while she was still healthy and before the MLD slowly took her away from us. "With a painting I will always be able to see Cal looking back at me," I told my sister Cathy, who patiently supported this request, though I discovered later that privately she feared it was evidence of my precarious mental state. The idea of wasting money on a painting as we faced years of caring for a medically complex child seemed foolish and reckless.

I work at Saint Joseph's University (SJU), which has a first-rate fine arts program, and my artist colleagues have a far higher tolerance of insanity than my own immigrant family of engineers and actuaries. Now I was on a noble quest to find the "finest portrait painter in Pennsylvania," and I reached out to them to recommend an artist for the job. "Money is no concern," I declared. A colleague, an internationally renowned photographer named Susan Fenton, responded to my request with a touching urgency. Of course, this portrait needed to be done immediately, Susan told me, and she had recommended only one person: her friend, a painter named Perky Edgerton.

Pat said nothing when I emptied thousands of dollars out of a small slush fund I kept for the children to commission a portrait. With Cal so ill he understood it was pointless to rein me in. And though neither of us could bear to say it out loud back then, Cal would not need money to purchase books for college. When my friends heard that I sold some jewelry to Joe the Jeweler (a guy on the back of buses promising cash for gold and silver) to subsidize the project, some of them quietly raised the rest of the money for me to pay for the portrait. Everyone seemed to understand that I had to get the painting done.

The moment I saw Perky's work, I knew I had found the woman who would capture my Cal. Most portrait painters are more craftsmen than artists, and they are asked to create an almost photographic likeness of their subjects. But Perky, who illustrates children's books, draws portraits that are far from literal. Her work is ethereal and beautiful and captures the essence of a child in all their complexity and uniqueness.

I explained to Perky over the phone that "my daughter was just diagnosed with leukodystrophy. There is a version that happens in toddlers—my daughter is two years old. She is dying and I need a painter to do her portrait while she still looks like herself." Perky was so moved by the commission that she told me not to worry about paying her all at once. She seemed to be even more careless and oblivious about money than I am. Anyone worried about getting paid would not be the right person to paint Cal. Here was a moment for beauty and art and generosity.

Cal's disease is cruel in so many ways. As it destroys the brain's white matter, it robs children of the light in their eyes. I wanted to find a painter who could forever preserve the way Cal would look at us with those brown eyes. I also wanted Perky to be sure the portrait included the parts of Cal's appearance that come from me. Of my three children, Cal resembles me the most in her coloring and hair. I clung to the idea that I needed to lock in her beauty. I also knew it was important to live with the painting while Cal was still alive; I didn't want the painting to be so sad that I would not be able to share it with others.

I met Perky just before her sixtieth birthday. Her ash-blond hair was streaked with white and, as her name suggests, she has the energy and affectation of an impish fairy rather than a woman of a certain age. At that first meeting Cal played around Perky's house and studio and sat on my lap to pose for photographs that Perky would need to do the portrait. We had an exceedingly (and maybe absurdly) normal visit given what I was there to do. Perky even said to me that Cal didn't look sick. I thought to myself that she clearly had not been around a two-year-old in a long time because someone who was used to toddlers would notice the issues with her gait, muscle tone, and lack of words. In a rare burst of patience, I assured Perky that despite appearances, Cal was in fact dying. "They are sending us on a Make-A-Wish trip next month," I said, as if that offered some irrefutable evidence that would convince her.

"I doubt I would have had the presence of mind to get my child's portrait painted in the midst of such news," Perky said. I liked her right away. She could see the practical and sensible in my deranged agony. I told her I believed that Cal was not really dying but was the Mermaid who could not live among humans because she was too precious and special. I hadn't shared this story with any of my friends or my husband or my parents. What Perky thought of this, I have no idea. But she listened and permitted me to share it without comment.

Getting Cal's portrait done was joyfully crazy. It was easy for me to be around Perky because she was not afraid to be around Cal or me. She joined me in the mania of needing to find meaning and beauty in the face of Cal's diagnosis. The portrait was my first lesson in how grief could be fashioned into beauty and art. This discovery would become my salvation.

Pat didn't want Camille and PJ to be haunted by the ghost of their sister and suggested we should have portraits of them done as well. But spending six thousand dollars on portraits was a bit excessive, even for me, and so we agreed to have Perky paint both of the girls.

To my relief and pleasure, Camille was intrigued and flattered by the idea of getting her portrait painted. I had worried that her twelve-year-old's self-consciousness would keep her from doing it. And so, as a belated present for my birthday, I kidnapped Camille and she sat in Perky's studio for the portrait. Camille was a natural. Perky's husband, Brian, who taught art at Swarthmore College, observed with a smile that she must have been an Italian aristocrat in a previous life since it was so easy for her to pose. I looked at Camille and searched for similarities to her baby sister. I could see the beauty of my youngest in her face and could imagine what Cal would have looked like had she been healthy and strong and able to grow up.

I took to calling the paintings of Cal and Camille "the girls," and as I left Cal's portrait with Perky so she could keep the two paintings in a visual conversation with each other, I heard myself tell Cal's portrait that her sister would take care of her while I was gone. I needed to say that Cal would not be alone, that her sister would watch out for her until I could come back and get them both.

Camille heard me, and I realized she might think my request was about more than just the paintings. Did I expect her to care for her sick and dying sister in real life? But I didn't need to ask; Camille already protected her little sister and understood that her father and I would need her help to get the family through this. What surprised her at Perky's studio was that I said it out loud.

I knew I had made the right decision about Cal's portrait when Perky brought it over for me to see. My mother and brother were visiting, and I had guessed that my mother, the most practical of women, would be troubled by the money I'd spent on it. Instead, when Perky uncovered the portrait, my mother gasped and started to cry. My brother smiled and turned away because he could not bear to look into Cal's eyes. They were like the eyes of the finest icons in the ancient monasteries in Greece, the ones that seem to follow you around the room.

Perky said, "I spent so much time on the eyes, and I changed the curls a bit, but it was the eyes. Did I get them right?" Of course, the fact that everyone was crying was proof that she had captured Cal's essence brilliantly.

Having Cal's and Camille's portraits done proved to be a lifesaving gift. To this day, when I speak to distraught parents of newly diagnosed children, I tell them about Perky and sitting for the portrait. Years later I learned that Barbara Bush had lost her three-year-old daughter, Robin, to leukemia. Over the years Mrs. Bush was regularly photographed surrounded by her living children and husband and with the oil painting of Robin hung above the mantel, watching over the family. It was strange that Mrs. Bush and I had shared this bond, that she had discovered the power of creating something beautiful and lasting out of grief.

It was a relief to know that I would always be able to have my Cal with me, staring back at me whenever I wanted or needed her.

THE FIFTH OF JULY

The countdown for our scheduled return to CHOP loomed large. Pat and I were barely speaking. It was like we had been in a terrible car wreck. He was in shock, but it seemed he had absorbed the blow in a way that allowed him to follow through with the routine of taking the kids to camp and making dinner. Grief had left me incapacitated. Fearing that my husband and children would be traumatized more if they knew how I longed to die with Cal, the best I could manage was to quarantine myself for fear of exposing others to my emotions.

Among the few people I spoke to over the ten days between Cal's diagnosis and our scheduled return to CHOP on the fifth of July were Elayna, who talked me through the science of Cal's disease and the prognosis. As an oral learner, I always preferred taking notes during a lecture over reading a paper. It was easier for me to understand MLD when Elayna was my guide. She talked, and I silently soaked it all in. One of the few questions I asked her was what she would do if Cal were her child. Elayna sighed and said, "I would think about leaving work so I could be with Cal while things are good."

I spoke with the clinical psychologist who had been working with me since Pat's diagnosis, Dr. Deborah Seagull, who texted me every few days as a virtual suicide watch. And I spoke with my neighbor Melissa Gale. Her children were the same ages as

Camille, PJ, and Cal. She had once shared with me that she lost her own mother when she was quite young and as a result quit her job as a nurse to be a full-time mother to her four children. When she returned to paid employment after her youngest son had enrolled in elementary school, she became a hospice nurse.

Melissa was one of the kindest, most compassionate women I knew. She offered me practical guidance about how to deal with the insurance companies, what to do about the feeding tubes, and how to find skilled nurses to work in our home. My phone calls with her were a crash course in what it would take to transform our home into a hospital. She gave me the confidence that I could be the mother Cal needed. Melissa assured me that "Cal will show you how to do this."

And there was Father Chris. As a young priest his first funeral had been for a child. Years before Cal's illness, when he'd shared that story in a homily, he had spoken with such honesty and authenticity about his sense of betrayal by a God who would make a child and a family suffer. Father understood he did not need to have all the answers and that it was just fine to say he had no comfort to provide besides his presence and the pledge that no matter what happened, I was not alone in this.

My instinct for self-preservation was clearly intact. I'd surrounded myself with people who understood the power of bearing witness to grief. What surprised me was that the brilliant people who had taught me, the professors from Oxford and other famous Ivy League schools, and the doctors we depended upon for medical advice were so useless in our crisis. One could argue (legitimately) that intellectuals consumed by the "life of the mind" tend to have deficits in emotional intelligence. But it was more than that. Most of them believed in the promise of science to manage suffering and pain. Physicians are laser-focused on conquering death and illness, but Cal's tragedy was a painful reminder of medicine's limits and the fallacy that human beings can control anything. During our time of need I could only stand to be around people who could help us face the inevitability of losing Cal and who understood how our heartbreak cast a shadow over everything in our lives.

O ur new routine of nonstop physical and occupational ther-apy, the nightmarish feeding clinic (where sick kids were forced to eat food they didn't want so their swallowing could be evaluated), and the meetings with social workers who tried their best but could say nothing that showed me a way for-ward had convinced me that there was no point in speaking to the doctors again. I understood Cal was dying and that all the treatments were painful, unproven, and experimental. There was nothing to be done but make Cal comfortable and enjoy the time we had left. I suspected I was the only person brave enough to face this truth.

My research online over the past few weeks had revealed that there were just three clinics, one at Duke University, one at Children's Hospital of Pittsburgh, and another at the Univer-sity of Minnesota, that treated children with MLD using bone marrow transplants. During Elayna's tutorials on leukodystro-phy, she had explained that for the past thirty years doctors had used bone marrow transplants to treat a range of mono-genic disorders (diseases caused by a single broken gene), such as the Bubble Boy disease, sickle cell anemia, and MLD.

Bone marrow transplants can save a leukemia or lymphoma patient's life by transplanting a healthy person's bone marrow into the patient, where it produces stem cells that are cancer free. Back in the 1980s doctors who specialized in bone mar-row transplants wondered if they could use the treatment for metabolic disorders such as MLD. The idea was to use chemo-therapy to eliminate all the old stem cells and allow the new bone marrow to reboot the patient's body with new stem cells that would be able to produce the missing enzyme. Bone mar-row transplants were effective with some metabolic disorders, but MLD moved too quickly, and only a few children who, like

Cal, had the most lethal form of the disease were ever considered eligible.

The biotech company Shire had recently launched a trial for an enzyme replacement therapy. Enzyme replacement therapy was an exciting possibility that had been a transformative treatment for similar disorders such as Pompe disease and MPS, two other rare enzyme-deficiency diseases. The study was in Brazil and required regular infusions for years. The work was promising, but it was in its early stages, and relocating to Brazil for the procedure was logistically impossible with Pat's cancer treatments and our older children. Years later, when I worked with families in clinical trials, I would be in awe of their willingness to sell their homes and cars and move across the country or the world to try experimental treatments that might save their children.

When I told Pat that I saw no point in returning to CHOP to meet the doctor, he said nothing. It was clear Pat wanted to speak with the doctors, but he would not force me to go with him. It was our friend and neighbor Peter Stein who offered a bit of tough love and insisted that we—Pat and I—had to go and listen to what the doctors had to say. Peter is a geriatrician and his wife, Kathleen, is an adult-hospice nurse. "With all due respect, Maria, I am not convinced that there is nothing they can do for Cal," Peter said. "You need to listen to them. These are the best people in the country." Besides, he noted, "you are pretty smart, but you are not a doctor."

The meeting was first thing in the morning. Pat dressed Callie in her prettiest outfit—a bright yellow dress with flowers and her white sandals. He and I didn't speak. I couldn't tell if he was annoyed or angry with me or indifferent. Peter arrived at the house and ushered me into the car. He had offered to come to the meeting with Dr. Waldman because he worried I would not go unless he escorted me into the building.

The neurology offices were located on the ninth floor at CHOP. Even though Cal was sick, she didn't look like the other patients in the waiting room, seated in wheelchairs, using feeding and tracheostomy tubes, and wearing helmets to protect their heads in case of seizures. Cal could still walk if we held her, and I recall staring at her and comparing her to the other children, still in utter disbelief that she was now one of the most seriously ill children in that room. A nurse called Cal's name, and we were whisked to a room at the far end of the building. You got the sense that these remote examination rooms were used for the difficult family meetings and the parents prone to outbursts. I wondered if there was a panic button hidden somewhere to alert security.

Back in 2012, even at the world-renowned Children's Hospital of Philadelphia, home to one of the nation's finest pediatric neurology programs, there was no one doing research on leukodystrophy in general or MLD specifically. Dr. Waldman worked with leukodystrophy patients because her specialty was multiple sclerosis, a myelin disorder like MLD.

In person Dr. Waldman was even younger than she appeared in her photo on the hospital's website. She wore a black suit, carried a Kate Spade purse, and bore more than a passing resemblance to the Facebook COO Sheryl Sandberg. She wore heels and perfect makeup. She was disarmingly charming; in other words, not what we had come to expect from a pediatric neurologist.

I had asked for someone from the chaplain's office to sit in on our meeting along with the social worker. Dr. Waldman's physical therapist, occupational therapist, and nurse practitioner wandered in and out of the meeting as well. A nurse appeared at the door at one point to tell Dr. Waldman that the resident assigned to shadow her that day had arrived. Through the opening of the door I could see a young man just shy of six feet tall standing in the corridor. He wore khakis and a freshly pressed blue oxford shirt. Dr. Waldman looked the young man up and down and announced, "No, no residents, fellows, or students for this one," as she closed the door in his face.

I liked Dr. Waldman immediately. Meeting a child with an ultrarare disorder such as MLD was a valuable teaching experience, but being truly present for a family like ours was not something she wanted to open up to an inexperienced doctor. From the start it was clear Dr. Waldman's focus was on Cal and Pat and me.

Dr. Waldman would be running this show, and her priority, after Cal, was me. She directed all her questions and answers and information to me, having figured out that I was the one who needed to be talked off the ledge. Pat clung to Cal like she was the only thing keeping him from falling down. He was absolutely silent, with an impenetrable poker face. I stared at Pat and forced myself to follow his lead. I was happy he wanted to hold Cal because I felt dizzy and lightheaded. It was difficult to breathe.

Dr. Waldman began, "I understand you don't want to pursue experimental treatments." There are, no doubt, some choice observations about me in Cal's folder, given that I had threatened the fellows with bodily harm if they took out their hammer on my kid one more time.

That's all it took. After having resisted coming to this meeting and having spent the days since Cal's diagnosis hardly speaking to my husband or children, I suddenly couldn't shut up. It was as if everything that I had kept locked in in me started to pour out and spill all over the floor. The lessons from Ms. Carol were discarded. This time it was about how I felt; it was my little girl who was sick.

Pat and Peter pushed their chairs so far up against the wall that they looked like twin spiders. All these words that I could not even remember formulating in my brain wanted to be heard. I was compelled in that moment to use every fiber of my being to empty my heart, so everyone in that room would see and hear me: "I have spent the last ten days listening to nurses, priests, neurologists, medical researchers, philosophers, and psychologists. I have listened to all of them and I understand that there is no proven treatment or cure." I said that I accepted that Cal was not a good candidate for a bone marrow transplant, that the disease had progressed too far. I didn't want to squander our good time in hospitals.

I turned to Pat and asked if what I said was right. It was my view of things, but since we had not spoken very much since Cal had been discharged, I could not even be sure Pat felt the same way I did. Pat's response was oddly formal, as if he were in a meeting being run according to Robert's Rules of Order: "I agree we are on the same page with this. I have nothing to add."

So I went on, crying so hard that I kept coughing to get air to speak. And the words kept coming. Dr. Waldman moved her chair next to mine and grabbed my hand tightly. She wept for my daughter with me and our family.

What I said next shocked everyone—my husband, Peter, the social worker, the nurse, and Dr. Waldman. Somehow, in the Oreo- and white-wine-fueled haze of the past ten days, I had formulated a way to cope, a strategy that compelled me to seek out some meaning and purpose in Cal's suffering. The words that flowed out of me felt like a vision or possibly a possession. And for a moment, instead of the rage and grief that had burned me up over those ten days, I found a path forward.

"Even though I am furious with God, it seems to me I understand the divine and the supernatural more clearly and forcefully than at any other moment in my life," I said. "I understand that God's love is not possible without suffering. I see this so clearly. I get it. I have spent the last several days since we left the hospital going to the pool and eating Goldfish crackers with Cal out in the sun. I now see how amazing and wonderful these things are."

This was the moment when I realized grief could be a superpower. My divine inspiration was the discovery that love could make weak and selfish people brave. When you unleashed all that you were feeling, you could tame your pain and harness it to do impossible things; you could be bold and fearless. Could this be how people changed the world? People who are content and comfortable do not change things. Progress requires people who are compelled to fight the status quo.

Now that the mermaid had revealed to me the very meaning of life, now that I could see the beauty and perfection in Cal, I felt I had to share what I had learned. Cal's legacy would be something extraordinary, even if we did not know what that could mean back then. Cal would make remarkable things possible; that day I was sure of it. While everyone else seemed frightened by my weeping and emphatic declaration, Dr. Waldman was willing to draw closer and listen intently. She was permitting herself to be infected by whatever delusional fever had infected me.

I turned to her and said, "I just want one thing now from medicine: I want to live long enough, Dr. Waldman, to see you all find a cure for this terrible disease. When you find the cure, I want you to find me, no matter where I am. I will get on a plane and go to Helsinki or Paris or wherever, and I want to meet the two-year-old girl you will save and see her mother's hope and gratitude that they will not have to endure what we have. And maybe, if I am really lucky, the little girl will have curls and huge brown eyes like my Cal. And I will weep for joy. And that's the only miracle I can hope for now."

I glanced at Pat and Peter. It looked as if they could have chewed off their own legs to escape. As the men pulled away, the social worker and the chaplain and Dr. Waldman seemed to draw closer. These women were mothers, you could tell— they understood and seemed moved by the clarity my grief had inspired.

I recognized that this was my moment. I was the only person in that room who had felt Cal grow inside of them. I had nursed her and felt her legs push up against my belly. I had been the one to give her brown eyes and curly hair and the genes that made it impossible for her to make the enzyme she needed to allow her brain to develop so she could grow and live. The paradox of me giving her life and passing on the genetic code that would be her death sentence was suffocating, and I forced it out of my mind with all of my strength. I knew that if it drilled down into my psyche it would kill me.

It was strange, but Dr. Waldman exhaled at the end of my speech. I asked her if they would ever cure MLD. She answered, "Oh yes, I truly believe we will." She continued, "The best hope is something called gene therapy, and I would say we are ten or twenty years away from that." I remembered something about a gene therapy trial in Italy, but I pushed it to the back of my mind.

Pat went off to speak to Dr. Waldman on his own. He would gradually reveal some details of their conversation over the next several weeks. In answer to all of our questions about how long Cal would live and how quickly she might lose the ability to walk, Dr. Waldman offered the same response: "No one knows what the future holds."

Dr. Waldman spent nearly two hours with us. She had a little girl at home named Arden, a bit younger than Cal. Arden had wavy hair and dark eyes just like Cal. I wondered if that might have been one of the reasons she spent so much time with us that morning.

Over the next several years, as Cal would return to the hospital and we would wonder if this was the moment when she would leave us, Dr. Waldman would visit us. She would come to the pediatric ICU or to celebrate Cal's birthday or Christmas or Thanksgiving or New Year's Day, often spending time with us after a twelve-hour shift before she went home to see her own children. She would sit by Cal's bedside or take me out to the upholstered chairs in the makeshift family room near the elevators on the PICU floor.

Throughout this time, Dr. Waldman came to see Cal as one of her own children. There was no pretense about professional distance. During her visits we would travel back to the day we met. To this day Dr. Waldman calls me on the fifth of July. She always tells me, "I don't think I can ever express to you how much Cal has changed my life, what your family has meant to me and my whole family, how much progress and hope exists now because of Cal. She has made so much good possible."

MAKE-A-WISH

By the end of July, after a summer spent bouncing between the hospital and the pool, we got word we would be going to Martha's Vineyard through Make-A-Wish. Once you are nominated for a Make-A-Wish trip, the organization reviews the case, assessing whether the child faces a life-limiting diagnosis. There are parents who actually pressure doctors to nominate them for the free vacation even when their child's illness is not life-threatening or life-limiting. Diseases such as lupus and cerebral palsy don't generally meet the standard that Make-A-Wish requires. With MLD there would be no issue. Cal easily met the life-limiting requirement.

Eligible children also must be older than thirty months and younger than eighteen. That children who are diagnosed as babies are not eligible for Make-A-Wish is understandably a sore point in the leukodystrophy community. MLD children generally get wishes, but children with an equally devastating form of the disease, Krabbe, who are typically diagnosed at six months and often do not survive beyond the age of three, did not. There could also be a fair bit of drama with Make-A-Wish over whether a current spouse rather than a biological parent could take the trip. Make-A-Wish Philadelphia once had to bail a father out of jail after he was arrested and detained on a trip to Disney World because of public intoxication and fighting.

The trip mostly filled me with dread, although the rest of my family was excited about it. Dr. Waldman, who called to check in on us regularly, encouraged us to do something magical. "I know most families go to Disney, but the thing is, you can always go to Disney. Make-A-Wish can grant a wish you could never do on your own." She told us about a family that had gone to the Vatican to see the pope. Pat, the collapsed Catholic, had no intention of squandering Cal's wish to spend time with priests and prayer.

At the time, Make-A-Wish Philadelphia could send a child and their family anywhere in the world for five days. Other than the fact that Make-A-Wish did not purchase business class tickets, there were hardly any restrictions put on the wishes besides advice about avoiding making requests of celebrities, who could be unreachable and problematic to work with on wishes. Our Make-A-Wish coordinator, Molly Giotto, told us about the boy who wished for a trip to Australia to swim along the Barrier Reef. Another girl had traveled to Paris and got a private shopping spree at Christian Louboutin. They had gifted the girl a pair of the famous red-soled shoes. (The girl returned the shoes, donating them back to Make-A-Wish to be auctioned off at their gala to fund another child's wish.) Other families used their wishes to create beauty rather than take a vacation. An MLD family in Pennsylvania, whose daughter was diagnosed not long after Cal was, used their wish to build a backyard garden so they could take their little girl, Loie, outside and listen to the birds and wind chimes. And a girl named Maddie Campbell, who had MLD, did something extraordinary and selfless with her wish.

MLD had ravaged the Campbell family; three of their five children had been diagnosed with the disease. Maddie, her sister Tori, and their younger brother Ike had all been diagnosed with a form of MLD that struck in adolescence. All three received bone marrow transplants. While Maddie and Ike recovered and their MLD seemed to become more indolent, Tori's treatment had come too late. She died less than two months before her eighteenth birthday.

All three siblings received bone marrow transplants at the University of Utah. Their parents, Aaron and Emily Campbell, shared their story through blogs and the local press.[1] As devout Mormons, they had traveled the world on missions, but they returned to the small town of Orem, Utah, for this ordeal. A bone marrow transplant is not a cure, but it can buy you time. While babies don't respond well, in older patients who can endure the risk of the transplant and who have a slower-moving form of the disease, a healthy donor's bone marrow can reboot their immune system with enough of the ARSA gene to produce the missing enzyme. As Maddie Campbell lay in the hospital for months in isolation and watched the other children fighting for their lives, she told her parents she wanted to do something for these kids. Rather than make the typical wish for a trip to Disney World or Hawaii, Maddie planned an event that was part birthday celebration and part service project. She wanted to share her wish with the entire community.

Her high school donated the use of its football stadium, and a local arts and crafts store provided thousands of dollars' worth of art supplies. Because the event was inspired by Maddie's family's time in China and the theme was "Girl on Fire," a Salt Lake City pyrotechnics club orchestrated a fireworks display. A professional event planner transformed the football stadium into an amusement park with bounce houses and "Girl on Fire" decorations. As a result, Maddie provided nearly two thousand craft kits to the Primary Children's Hospital.

Make-A-Wish prefers to interview children before a holiday is chosen. It wants to make sure kids are not being coerced into making wishes their parents want. It was astounding to think that there were parents who would take over a child's wish, but apparently it was not uncommon. Since Cal lacked the language to express her wishes, Pat and I were her voice.

Cal was happiest in the water, so we knew that's what the trip would involve. Because she was getting weaker and Pat was still undergoing chemotherapy, it would be too much for us to travel overseas, so we decided on Martha's Vineyard. Pat had found the Winnetu Oceanside Resort on the internet. While most hotels are not as wonderful as they look in their brochures, the Winnetu is the opposite—the photos did not come close to suggesting the beauty of the place.

You might think I would be looking forward to an all-expenses-paid trip to Martha's Vineyard, but I detested the idea. I wasn't ungrateful. The Make-A-Wish Foundation is a great organization, but this isn't a group of people you want entering *your* life, because that happens only if you have a sick or dying child. When they came by to deliver our tickets and the money for our trip, with the carefully prepared packet with Calliope's name decorated in glitter and a picture of her favorite PBS character, Kipper, on the cover, I didn't want to answer the door. Would it be possible for me to turn off the lights and pretend we were not home? Part of me wanted to yell at them to get out of my house, and the kinder they were the more furious I felt myself becoming. It was the crazy, out-of-control rage I imagine rampage shooters have when they open fire on a room full of people they don't even know. In those moments when you feel so much pain and disappointment, you want to make everyone else around you feel the world's horror and brutality with you. And for an instant I could imagine the headlines: "Crazed Grieving Mother Murders Make-A-Wish Representative."

The woman from Make-A-Wish also brought over some gifts for Cal: a Make-A-Wish T-shirt, a Make-A-Wish tote bag, and a Make-A-Wish Barbie doll. She explained that Make-A-Wish gives all the boys Make-A-Wish Matchbox cars and all the girls get Barbies. The debit card we used on our trip had the Make-A-Wish logo on it underneath Bank of America's branding. I kept thinking about the twentysomething marketing whiz kid from Syracuse who sat in on the meeting at Mattel suggesting they brand a charity for seriously ill children. Like Mattel needs to corner the sick-and-dying-kid demographic. The Barbie was wearing a pink-and-gold tutu—Pat hypothesized that she was meant to look like a fairy—and she looked far too healthy. She should at least have a wheelchair or be missing her hair from chemotherapy and radiation. There was no way in hell I was putting the Make-A-Wish T-shirt on Cal. I also didn't plan to use that bag at the supermarket anytime soon.

MLD was making Cal weaker and sicker by the day. She was deteriorating quickly, and Make-A-Wish had been advised by the medical team that the trip needed to be fast-tracked because she could start experiencing seizures and would soon need a feeding tube. Once kids start to show symptoms of the disease, they lose everything. And Dr. Waldman worried a trip might be impossible if we waited too long. But this meant that the newness of Cal's diagnosis and our grief were so raw that it was difficult for us to find a way to enjoy a vacation that was possible only because Cal was dying.

It was more difficult than I had first imagined to explain the trip to Martha's Vineyard to our older children. Camille understood that Make-A-Wish was for sick and dying children, and she shared my ambivalence about this charity. It was PJ who saved the trip for all of us. He seemed to think going on a Make-A-Wish trip was like winning a prize on a television game show.

Cal's diagnosis had made PJ the master of magical thinking. It is more than likely that he inherited these tendencies from my father and me. Even before Cal's diagnosis, my dad and I possessed this deep belief in our capacity to will the world to bend to our vision of how things were supposed to be. In adults such magical thinking might be rightly seen as delusional and self-aggrandizement, but PJ's was developmentally appropriate and a handy coping strategy. His amnesia about Cal's prognosis

made him excited about Martha's Vineyard and somehow gave
us permission to look forward to it as well

Make-A-Wish has an undeniable flair. A white limousine
picked us up at the house on the day we flew to Providence. I
had never been in a white limousine for prom or for our wedding, and taking one because Cal was sick felt surreal. We were
greeted by Make-A-Wish volunteers all along the trip, and the
Massachusetts Make-A-Wish chapter was so honored to have
been selected as a wish destination that a volunteer greeted us
in person at the airport to make sure we found our limo to
Woods Hole, where we would catch the ferry to Martha's Vineyard, and that we were all fine.

Make-A-Wish wanted to arrange for photo-ops and have
us carry water bottles to announce who we were and why we
were taking this vacation, but, uncharacteristically, this was a
time when I wanted to stay below the radar. I wanted to allow
Cal to pass for a little while longer as a healthy child.

We were greeted at the hotel by the manager and led to the
most extravagant cottage at the resort. It had a kitchen, a sitting room, three bedrooms, and a washing machine and dryer.
When we checked out, we would learn that the cottage rented
for two thousand dollars a day. The hotel had provided a crib
for Cal and towels, a wagon, lawn chairs, and T-shirts for the
whole family. A tray of warm chocolate-chip cookies awaited
us in the kitchen and there was a sign welcoming Cal and her
family. Our windows overlooked a lawn full of wild roses and
offered a view of the clear Vineyard sky. At night we were awe-
struck by the stars—Pat and I hadn't seen stars like this since
our vacation to Maine back in 2002.

The trip was our first family vacation since 2003 and the
only nice one Pat and I have had since our honeymoon. Our
vacations usually were visits home to see our respective parents in Boston or Ireland or travel mooched off conferences
to San Francisco and DC. This was the first and final time Cal
would be on a plane. It would also be the last time she would

travel to Cape Cod, a place that had defined my childhood so profoundly.

My father and mother had not wanted to intrude on our trip. Mom made excuses for not visiting, saying Dad's chemotherapy meant he wasn't well enough to travel. It seemed to me that the news that Cal was dying had unraveled my father. His famous optimism had been replaced by a truculent despair, and he would rage at me when I said Cal was terminally ill and dying. I had started to believe that Pat had been right to keep the truth from his parents about how sick Cal was. The truth was that Dad could not bear to face what the disease was doing to her. He would never see her after her diagnosis.

Martha's Vineyard is simply one of the most beautiful places on the planet, and seeing it from the view of a luxury resort on South Beach makes you understand why movie location scouts regularly choose it for films about impossibly perfect people. For people like Pat and me, who grew up near the ocean, Martha's Vineyard would be our location scout's choice for our cinematic version of heaven. There was a point one day when I was lying in the bed between Cal and Pat, who were both asleep. I thought to myself that if I believed in some afterlife and imagined that heaven was a place where I would be reunited with all the people I missed and loved, this was the scene I would describe. When I considered that this wonderful joy of sleeping next to the two of them would not be possible in a fast-approaching future, it was profound and overwhelming, an excruciatingly painful version of joy.

It was nearly impossible not to be enchanted by the Vineyard. We spent all day in the water. PJ had been signed up for a day camp program and had made friends with the sons and daughters of hedge fund and biotech CEOs who could afford to summer for a week or two at the Winnetu. Many of the guests did not know what to make of our family, who were wearing Old Navy bathing suits but staying in the most expensive accommodations at the resort.

The first night, Pat and I, trying to have a grown-up night out, went to an expensive restaurant, and I ordered salmon with vegetable risotto. I took a few bites and it was delicious but then I remembered why I was sitting in this restaurant and eating this forty-dollar entrée and I started to gag. The salmon had been transformed into something vile and awful. No more fancy restaurants on Make-A-Wish; from that day on I shared Cal's macaroni and cheese dinners, and my stomach was just fine.

The other extremely challenging part was the mothers and fathers with the exquisitely healthy two-year-olds. I was mesmerized by these children but appalled that so many of the parents were texting or using cell phones while their toddlers learned to swim in the pool or were carted off to day camp. I hated those parents, envious that they could take these things for granted. At the same time, I missed being one of those parents who didn't see the wonder in a healthy child. Watching their children talk and walk and run and smile and use their hands made me see what a delicate little bird my Cal had become. At CHOP she looked healthy and strong, but here at the resort her sickness was incredibly clear. The decline over the past few months was undeniable.

A little boy named Jack, who had just turned two in June, adored Cal and tried to touch her hair and kiss her. Jack's mother noticed that her son seemed more developmentally advanced than Cal despite the fact that he was six months younger. She graciously remarked that Cal must still be tired from her journey. I was grateful for the woman's kindness and played along with our pretend game of the sleepy Cal, but she could see that there was something very wrong. I really did love seeing Jack, who was so smart and handsome and quick and could run up the stairs to his hotel room and give me high-fives. We were best friends by the time we left, but I would hide and cry somewhere no one could see me after we shared our moments together. Jack reminded me so much of PJ and my nephew John.

It felt bizarre to be Make-A-Wish celebrities, but it was moving how consistently people went out of their way to be kind. The rental company that provided us with Cal's high chair and crib and wagon for getting her to the beach insisted we did not have to pay. The resort's photographer spent an hour trying to do our family portrait and took at least two hundred dollars off her standard fee, and the manager wanted to feature one of the photographer's pictures of my lovely Cal in their new brochure. When I mentioned that I wanted to get some Chilmark Chocolates as a gift for a friend, the assistant manager offered to drive to the other side of the island on her day off to get me some. The survey I filled out made the staff cry, and they handed back the tip we left for them. The one thing I had mastered in the weeks and months after Cal's diagnosis was my ability to make people cry. Pat and I promised the hotel staff and ourselves we would return, but we never did.

During our Vineyard vacation I realized that I don't fear dying anymore. I don't want to live to be old; the idea of being around until my nineties holds no appeal. I am not afraid of flying on planes or climate change. The only things that scare me are losing Cal and Pat. I can't decide what is worse: losing Cal or being on my own to face her death without Pat. Denial is an essential part of my survival strategy and losing Pat is just unimaginable to me.

So I simply refused to accept what the doctors said about Pat's cancer. He will not leave me when he is fifty-seven. He will get to see his son and daughter finish college and fall in love and have lives of their own. Pat will do so well he may even outlive me—especially if I keep eating so much and putting on weight. Pat will have enough time to raise our children and will be there for his parents and Cal.

In my mind, Pat, PJ, and Camille are protected because our tragedy has earned them a long life of good health and good fortune. I am not sure what it means that I have envisioned a world without Cal but not without Pat. It is pure selfishness but, more generously, self-preservation. The only way I did not succumb to my grief about Cal is because of the promise to myself that Pat would be okay.

The Monday we flew back to Philadelphia it was raining on the Vineyard, maybe to help us let go of this beautiful place and transition back to doctors' appointments and physical therapy and worrying about bills and feeding clinics. On the Vineyard, Pat and I got on the same page about Cal's disease. It had already won, so we agreed we would be focused on making her life—and our lives—as beautiful as possible. We would not go to the hospital unless we needed to; a good day would be spent watching movies and reading books and swimming in the pool. One of the most important lessons of Martha's Vineyard had been to recognize and appreciate the perfection of holding Cal and just being with our children.

Sometimes I wondered if I was supposed to have Cal in my life to learn a different way of looking at the world, to see the perfection of her divine love, gifts that do not require words and which must be condensed into such a short life. My wonderfully wise and kind friend Scott Charles, who works at Temple University Hospital's trauma center and treats children and adults ripped apart by car crashes and stab wounds and bullets, offered a different explanation. He wondered if it occurred to Pat and me that Cal was lucky to have us as parents. The fact that she is so joyful despite this terrible disease was in no small part because Pat and I were her parents, he believed, and we shouldn't underestimate how much our love saved her.

I have to admit that made me feel better. So maybe if Cal had to have a life like this, her blessing would be to have Pat and Camille and PJ and me take care of her and be there for this. Cal surely doesn't see her life as a tragedy. She accepts what is and smiles and laughs every day.

Instead of going to CHOP the day we returned home, I wrote a letter to Make-A-Wish. I confessed how I had not wanted to take the trip, how it had seemed wasteful and even obscene to have a dream vacation because Cal was going to die. The Barbies and the T-shirts and the limos had all seemed ridiculous. And yet the trip had been "my version of heaven on Earth. Martha's Vineyard is a place I will return to again and again." I told them, "I will never forget what you have done for our family, and this time away has transformed all of us. I think you made it easier for us to face what is coming."

All these years later, when I have sat in a pediatric ICU and watched Cal and my family endure so much pain and suffering, the place I dream of and hold on to and transport myself to is the sea at Martha's Vineyard and sleeping with Cal and Pat beside me on that bed.

MEDICAID

At CHOP, the nurses and doctors and therapists all address mothers of the patients they're treating simply as "Mom." Most doctor's visits are managed by mothers, and the clinicians cannot possibly remember all the names of the parents they meet. For mothers of children like Cal, Mom is a formal title, a designation that is a mark of respect and deference, the way you might address a doctor or a priest. For the mothers of children with rare diseases such as MLD, our expertise about our kids' care rapidly overtakes what the experts know about the disease.

We were back at the hospital for one of our follow-ups that August, right before our trip to Martha's Vineyard. Chrissy, one of the therapists who had seen Cal on the fifth of July when we met Dr. Waldman, could not hide her concern at how much thinner and weaker Cal had become over the course of just one month. Her tremors were more severe, and she would hold her hands in clenched fists. Looking at Dr. Waldman's face, I knew things were going as badly as I feared. When she suggested getting Cal braces for her hands because they were curving in, I called Dr. Waldman.

Dr. Waldman spoke to Pat the next day and said that maybe they hadn't caught the MLD as early as they'd thought. Dr. Waldman wanted Cal to have more nursing, perhaps a feeding tube, and also a referral to hospice. Dr. Waldman agreed that speech therapy was not "worth it"—more visits to the doctor only increased the risk of infection. And she told Pat, "Cal is never going to walk or speak again."

Dr. Waldman had come to agree with my assessment of the situation: the braces and standers and therapy that forced Cal to walk were failing. Cal liked aqua therapy, but the weekly sessions of physical and occupational therapy were painful and futile. Dr. Waldman thought we might want to move away from "stopping the MLD" and redirect our efforts to "managing the symptoms," shifting to a palliative care model with hospice.

I had assumed this for a while and was relieved that Dr. Waldman was brave enough to tell us the truth. I knew Cal was drooling more, had trouble sitting in her stroller, and could no longer hold up her head. But Pat was still processing things. Sometimes he did not see Cal as a child with a terminal illness; he clung to the idea that she had special needs and was disabled. My desire to protect him and the kids from how badly things were going had left them ill prepared to get this news.

After the doctors told us Cal would never grow up, every fiber of my being went into caring for this baby. I tried to do the heavy lifting of managing her care, rationalizing that Pat shouldn't go to hospitals given how chemotherapy compromised his immunity. The real reason, though, was that I *needed* to care for Callie. When the doctor suggested that we could get nursing help since we were eligible for four hours per day, I was incredulous. No one else could do it like I could. I am not a saint, but this is just a statement of fact: no one takes care of Cal like I do.

Cal's prognosis had convinced me I would fail her as a mother if I did anything except hold her and be with her. It seemed to me an abdication of my maternal duties if I left her with other people. We had to make memories and it was a sin not to spend every waking moment with her. It did not matter if my marriage or my other children or my job or my own health suffered. All that mattered was my Cal.

Not surprisingly, this had rather significant implications for how my other children were mothered during this time. I was MIA; the more generous interpretation was that I was having a nervous breakdown and needed to keep them at a safe distance to protect them from the fallout, and that it would have caused irrevocable harm if I had exposed them to an unfiltered version of my grief. The whole family was drowning, but until I could save myself I couldn't help others. I prayed they could get along well enough without me for a while.

This meant they faced their grief on their own. Years later Camille would confront me about how I had lost my mind in the weeks and months after Cal's diagnosis. This was true; there was no point in denying it. Maybe Camille had intended for me to fight with her, so when I answered, "Yes, I did go crazy," she appeared relieved that her version of events aligned with mine. If I could tell her the truth about this time, maybe she could believe me now when I promised, "But now, I am better."

In between the rolling nervous breakdowns that summer, a good deal of my time was devoted to fighting with insurance companies and Medicaid. It was surreal to find ourselves at war with nameless bureaucrats at insurance companies, in billing departments, at medical supply companies, and in the county welfare office who seemed inconvenienced by how much money our heartbreak would cost them. Most people would be surprised to learn that one of the first things you must do when you learn your child has a terminal illness is enroll in Medicaid. During a visit to the hospital not long after Cal's diagnosis, a social worker pulled Pat and me aside and urged us to start the paperwork. This surprised me. "We have great insurance," I assured her. "Why do we need Medicaid?"

The social worker smiled, almost charmed by my naiveté, and insisted, "Oh, you are going to need this, honey."

Medicaid would become the focus of my ire that summer. It is best known as the health insurance program for poor families, but it also serves as supplementary insurance for families whose kids get sick. In America, when a child has a disease such as MLD, it is not simply a tragedy. It is also an economic disaster. Even people who have two good incomes and health insurance will find themselves under water pretty fast. If you think it's expensive to go to the hospital, try transforming your house into one. Private health insurance does not cover the three-thousand-dollar custom-built stroller, the bath chair, or the dozens of hours of work by skilled nurses and aides that would be required if we were to return to our jobs. When I realized I would have to go to war with the government when my kid was dying, it was like being dropped into a dystopian alternative reality. And this in the richest country in the world.

President Ronald Reagan fundamentally transformed Medicaid because of a little girl named Katie Beckett. When she was just five months old, Katie contracted viral encephalitis, a brain infection, and went into a coma. After recovering she had partial paralysis that left her unable to breathe without a ventilator for much of the day. Medicaid would pay for the expensive treatment only if she stayed in the hospital. In 1981 Reagan heard about her situation and changed the rule so she could go home. The administration was looking for ways to balance the budget, and in a rare intersection of fiscal conservativism and human kindness, the Reagan administration noted it would cost significantly less—about one-sixth as much—for Katie to receive care at home instead of in a hospital. Today nearly half of the nation's thirteen million sick and disabled children receive Medicaid or are covered by the Children's Health Insurance Program (CHIP), and a good deal of this money is spent to ensure they can live at home.

What most people don't realize is that Medicaid is best understood as fifty-one different insurance programs controlled by the fifty states and the District of Columbia. While Medicare is managed by and gets its funding from the federal government, it is administered by the states. As a result, it is to a state's advantage to make the application process as arbitrary and arduous as possible so that fewer patients enroll. After all, the simplest way to keep health-care costs down is to keep people from receiving care. Depending on where you live, getting health care for your sick kid ranges from the challenging to the Sisyphean. Fortunately for us, we live in Pennsylvania, one of the handful of states where a diagnosis of MLD means you are automatically eligible for Medicaid. Doctors at CHOP actually tell out-of-state patients to relocate to Pennsylvania to take advantage of its Medicaid program.

The result is that states with good coverage are burdened with more high-need families, putting more strain on the system. By 2019, Cal had had 1,712 documented encounters with providers, 194 blood tests, 42 X-rays, 22 ER visits, 16 admissions (including two to the PICU), 11 ultrasounds, and 2 MRIs. Her care at the Children's Hospital of Philadelphia has cost $1.1 million. This does not include the cost of ninety-six hours a week of skilled nursing, her twelve medications, the special formula for her G-tube that costs $200 per case, diapers, medical equipment that gets shipped to our home, and our home-based care. A more accurate estimate is probably around $2 million.

Fifty percent of children with Cal's disease don't make it to their fifth birthday. Cal turned ten in 2019. When people wondered how she had beaten the odds, I would say it was because she lives in Pennsylvania. It is because of Medicaid. In Indiana, for instance, and many other Medicaid-unfriendly states, families with a kid like Cal might wait months or even a year to get coverage. That means a family is cashing out savings accounts and 401(k)s to get their child a wheelchair or pay for medications and physical therapy. In a large number of states Medicaid kicks in only with hospice and end-of-life care.

Part of me relished the idea of a fight with the Montgomery County Department of Welfare. I now had a worthy adversary for my rage and grief. The first stage of my campaign required submitting our application in person. I was tempted to bring Cal to the welfare office with me but decided against it given how difficult it was for her to travel and not knowing how long I would need to be there. Montgomery County, which includes Philadelphia's Main Line, has one of the highest concentrations of millionaires in the United States, up there with Silicon Valley and Manhattan. But there are poor people here, too, and the Montgomery County Welfare office sits in a shabby storefront at a strip mall and looks just like the welfare offices across City Avenue in Philadelphia.

In line at the welfare office I stood out because I had no child in tow with me that day. Though no one made any remarks, it was surreal to be wearing work clothes I had purchased at Nordstrom and to be carrying my two-hundred-fifty-dollar Tory Burch purse. If someone from Fox News had walked by, they could have attacked me for being a leech on society. Most of the women standing in line for Medicaid, or other state and federal assistance programs such as TANF, WIC, and food stamps, have no husband or partner to watch over their children. They certainly don't have money to pay a sitter. As I waited for my number to be called, I expected someone to ask why I was there, but people were distracted by their own children and their own woes. Here was a place where sorrow and misfortune were mundane and banal.

When I did finally get up to the counter to submit my paperwork, I worked into the conversation that my daughter was quite sick and that we would need our application expedited. The quiet, sad-eyed woman waiting on me looked up, catching my eyes for the first time. In a place where hearing stories from mothers who could not feed, clothe, or shelter their children was part of the job description, you needed to keep a safe distance. But even here, at the Department of Welfare, next door to a city with the highest concentrations of poverty, opioid overdoses, and gun violence in the nation, my story rose above the rest.

"Cal is not just sick; she is dying," I explained. "The doctors say she has just three years to live. We are going on our Make-A-Wish holiday soon and the social worker at CHOP tells me we need Medicaid as quickly as possible so we can get Cal into physical and occupational therapy and get her a new stroller." It was hard to say if this was working; maybe I had overplayed my hand and said too much. The woman took it all in and said, "I am sorry, I will pray for a miracle for your daughter."

I nodded and thanked her. I did nothing to correct the woman's faith that Cal could "beat" MLD. I was getting used to people telling me they would pray for Cal to "get a miracle." After Cal got sick, people who did not like doctors and science would offer to introduce me to healers who would cure her with a gluten-free diet and CBD oil or to ministers who would lay hands on her to save her. Grief made some people believe in angels and go online to find people who could save their children with a gene therapy available only in China, but that was not me. Grief made me angry, fat, and impatient with kind people who advised me to pray for a miracle. I believed the doctors. I accepted that Cal was dying and that no one defeats MLD; there is no coming back from a dead neuron. The only miracle I wanted that day was a Medicaid approval. And my strategy for achieving this goal—emotional blackmail—seemed like it would work.

So even though it made me wince, I understood that the welfare worker's line about praying for Cal was an opening, a flash of pity and vulnerability. This was a moment of weakness for anyone working at the welfare office. So, like a lion that had drawn blood, I went in for the kill and pulled out my phone to show her a photo of Cal smiling at the pool. The worker looked down without any noticeable emotional response and said, "She doesn't look sick." This was also something I heard a great deal that summer. "It's neurological," I explained. "She can't walk or speak. She is sicker than she looks right now."

It was surreal to boast about how sick Cal was, but it worked. Whispering so that her supervisor could not hear our conversation, the worker handed me a piece of paper: "Here is Mrs. Coleman's direct line. If I were you, I would call her to follow up." Boom, the keys to the castle. The name and direct phone number of a supervisor managing Cal's case would be the way to jump ahead of the line! The woman could no doubt have been reprimanded, or worse, for giving out a supervisor's direct line to a deranged mother.

Over the next month, every day of the week, from Monday to Friday, at 11:30 a.m., I called Mrs. Coleman. Each time I left the same message. "My name is Maria. I am calling for my daughter Calliope Carr, birthday 12/23/09. My daughter has a terminal illness with a three-year life expectancy, and we need Medicaid as soon as possible. Thank you for your time." She never answered the phone, and no one ever returned my call. I dreaded making those calls, and I would always do it hidden in my bedroom so the children and Pat would not overhear me in case someone did pick up the phone.

Every time I said those words into the phone it seemed as if I was cutting open my chest cavity. But it also made me feel powerful. My mother and husband winced when I used the "d-word," and they asked me not to do so. But the word gave me a way to get what I needed. Saying Cal was dying weaponized my grief. Not all parents could calmly set out to make other people feel as terrible as I did, but I was on a mission. The father of another MLD child much preferred the euphemisms "passed away" or "lost her battle." He had never used the d-word even after his daughter had succumbed to MLD in his arms. But for me, a phrase like "getting angel wings" trivialized our pain and, worse, was imprecise and inaccurate. And in moments when you are fighting the government, the d-word, with all its power and pain, was the nuclear option.

I was not exaggerating when I told Mrs. Coleman how important Medicaid was. Pat told me our insurance had rejected a number of Cal's medical bills already, and if we were going to get her aqua therapy and new equipment and keep up with the growing number of medications she needed, the approval could not come quickly enough. Cal's Medicaid approval just arrived in the mail one day. You would have no sense that this unremarkable letter exacted so much effort and anguish.

That summer of Cal's diagnosis our home would be transformed into a hospital. The approval of our application for Medicaid meant we now had forty hours per week of nursing care. This altered our lives dramatically. We would be able to leave the house and return to our jobs, get to the supermarket, or watch Camille's and PJ's track meets and know Cal was being cared for.

Maggie Strang, a nursing supervisor with the home healthcare company Bayada, first appeared at our home not long after the Medicaid approval. Along with Maggie were two hospice nurses from Abington Hospital, Karen and Ellen. Abington Hospital is home to one of the nation's four in-patient children's hospice units. With Cal's referral to hospice and the approvals from Medicaid, Abington and Bayada would be evaluating our medical equipment and nursing needs. It would be Maggie's job to identify and hire nurses and aides who were a good fit for Cal and our family. Medicaid would cover these services because Pat and I would need help to return to work. Karen and Ellen would interface with the hospice team and the medical team at CHOP's Pediatric Advanced Care Team and would be the eyes and ears for Cal's doctors at CHOP. The goal was to keep her comfortable, stable, and at home and out of the hospital.

Cal had access to medical care 24/7 even when the nurses were not working, and Karen and Ellen could be dispatched to assess her in an emergency. There was a team at CHOP that would meet weekly to track how Cal was doing and to discuss any changes and developments in her care. It was both a relief, and somewhat terrifying, to realize how many different people were going to be involved in her care. There was no way to avoid seeing how serious this was. Cal's disease would require dozens of people coordinating with our whole family to get through it.

Maggie, Karen, and Ellen were all in their fifties and early sixties, seasoned nurses with years of experience, and all three exuded quiet confidence. It astounded me that they had cared for children like Cal for decades. All three women had started their nursing careers in the 1980s at CHOP. They had worked in oncology and in the ICU, and seeing children die was not something they had grown numb to, but it was something they understood.

In-patient nursing at a place such as CHOP is a prestigious job, but it is also stressful and demanding, and after decades of managing the grueling schedules, Maggie, Karen, and Ellen had made the shift to home-based care, as many experienced nurses with families of their own do. It astounded me that they would still choose to be around families like ours and children like Cal, but we learned quickly that all three of them could see the beauty in Cal.

They complimented us on our one-hundred-year-old house with its original oak door and brass fixtures and the wild gardens and raised vegetable beds out front. Maggie joked that it looked like it belonged to professors. They had Googled Pat and me, and Maggie praised us for the articles we had published and the books we had written. They spoke about their experience working with families on welfare and Medicaid, and they were eager to discuss my research. While the woman

I used to be would have basked in their praise, the new version of me had no time for such things.

The nurses wanted to know about our routine with Cal. They took detailed notes about how she preferred to sit on Pat or me. They learned that to help her gain weight I fed her eggs soaked with butter and covered in melted cheese or Oreos soaked in milk. I rattled off the calories in all her favorite meals and lamented that while Cal was losing weight I was packing on the pounds. They took note of Cal's drooling and of the facts that she could no longer drink water or milk and that unless her food was thickened to just the right consistency she would choke. They asked about how often we gave her Valium for pain or a laxative to move her bowels. They asked about seizure activity and I noted that she had none. When I explained that some but not all kids with MLD have seizures because the damage to the brain—the demyelination—does not always lead to actual seizures but sometimes to seizure-like activity, the nurses were impressed that I understood the difference between the two.

I saw the nurses notice the toys neatly piled in the corner, untouched. How relieved I was that they did not ask about them. They wanted to know if Cal could use the toilet or say any words at all, and my heart sank as I answered no to both questions. But I wanted them to know that Cal was very much aware of her surroundings and that I suspected that the experts who told us she had dementia or was in a coma were wrong. I believed that kids who were said to be in a coma were really being overmedicated. Cal was still so bright and alive. She was not going anywhere, I said.

The nurses smiled and nodded and wrote down what I said. I told them I was upset that I needed help to care for Cal, that it felt like a failure and a disappointment. They held my hand and said, "We are here to help. You are a wonderful mother. Your daughter knows how much you love her. We are just here to help." They embraced me as I wept. It was nice to have someone hold my hand and let me be scared without trying to make me hide how I felt. The wonderful thing about having the nurses in our lives was that they could witness what was happening and knew that the only thing to say was "You don't have to do this on your own." No one tried to tell me to be brave or stop crying or stop being scared.

Our home hospital created a new division of labor. When he was not in treatment Pat devoted all his energies to keeping Camille and PJ busy with camp and friends and soccer and basketball. He was on the front lines battling to reclaim our sense of normalcy. My job that summer was to manage Cal's care, fight with Medicaid, and deal with the doctors at CHOP. My mothering approach for my older children had always been rather laid-back compared with the other Main Line moms. A size-16 college professor with untamed, curly hair, I was not like the stylish size-00 women who would come to the soccer games wearing Lululemon.

While I enjoyed watching Camille and PJ play basketball and soccer, Pat had been their coach and had devoted every weekend to traveling with the teams and managing the drama among both the kids and the parents. Pat had coached Camille and PJ since they were four, and he had already looked into registering Cal for Lower Merion Soccer and Main Line Girls Basketball when she was older. Despite the fact that I have no interest in sports (and even less ability), our older children were talented athletes with a religious devotion to sports. Of all the things Pat lost with Cal, the chance to watch her play sports and be her coach was one of the biggest for him.

Pat was stronger, almost back to normal. The only allowances he made to cancer were the weekly infusions. And the only obvious sign of the disease was that he had shrunk two inches because the lesions in his spine had caused fractures in his back that made him shorter. Whatever fears and anxieties Pat had about being diagnosed with cancer at forty-five years old he kept mostly to himself. But there was one night that summer, not long after Cal's diagnosis, when it all seemed to be getting to him. We were watching TV together and it was late. Cal was in bed, but it was hot and the air conditioner was keeping us both up because it was noisy and not cooling off the house. Without warning Pat suddenly said, "What if something happens to me? How can you take care of the children?"

I was surprised and startled. This was one of the few times in our years together that Pat had exposed any vulnerability or worry about the future. Since he has no patience for lies or false hope, I wanted to find the right words to offer encouragement without denying the seriousness of everything. He was sitting in a leather armchair, and I got off the couch and kneeled next to him. Wrapping my arms around his waist, I whispered in his ear, "You are the most amazing father. You are taking care of us. You are not going anywhere anytime soon, I promise." Pat nodded and fought back the emotion trying to escape. It seemed to work. Pat's cancer was not going to be cured, Cal was not going to get better, but all I knew was that neither one of them was going to die soon, and that had to be enough.

That summer I did not ration out screen time for Camille and PJ or insist they eat their vegetables. One day Camille was watching an R-rated movie, and I said nothing. PJ would go to the basement and play Minecraft on his Xbox until he fell asleep in front of the TV. Camille would spend hours, unsupervised, on her computer and had started cooking for herself. PJ would somehow have a stash of money and had the number to his favorite pizza places memorized. When food hadn't been brought over by the church or the neighbors, it seemed perfectly fine for them to eat a bowl of cereal or order a pizza for dinner.

While Pat was doing better, Cal's disease seemed to be moving at lightning speed. It was like she had fallen off a cliff. Dr. Waldman said she would likely stabilize, but for the first few months after MLD is diagnosed the disease tends to "make itself known." Cal lost everything. At Easter she was falling and struggling with her gait. Now it took hours for her to carefully swallow the smoothies I prepared. Sitting up on her own had become challenging; she would topple over if you did not sit behind her.

In August, Cal uttered her final word. She looked up at Pat, her face beaming and her eyes bright, and said, "Daddy." It was said with such emotion and love. The desire to call his name had been so powerful she had willed her body to push through the broken nervous system and damage to her brain to make the word come out of her mouth. To hear her speak was magic, completely unexpected. Cal's "Daddy" had a singsong quality; it sounded like a chiming clock: Daadee. Pat and I froze when she said it. We knew, at the time, that it would be the last word she spoke, and we were not sad so much as grateful for the gift that it was, a gift so filled with pure, sweet love for her father.

The strategy for caring for Callie resembled what you would do for a newborn: watching for the trinity of eating, sleeping, and pooping. And if you don't do all three, you lose and lose big. How miserable are any of us when we cannot eat, sleep, or poop? When people asked how I was doing I would tell them about what Cal had eaten, or how well she had slept, or the color and consistency of her poop. Pat and I would text each other updates on Cal throughout the day about what she was eating and how her gas was.

The same energy I devoted to writing books and professional pursuits was now put toward creating food for Cal to eat. Much to my amazement Whole Foods did not carry prune juice, so I wrote a letter to the customer service department. Since Cal was having trouble swallowing, I took to puréeing everything: chicken parmesan, salmon, risotto, and rice pudding. One time I tried to purée a Wendy's hamburger. It was a total disaster. Our pantry was filled with Oreos, Pop-Tarts, and doughnuts, anything that was caloric—Michelle Obama would have staged an intervention.

Yet Cal was losing so much weight that she would need a feeding tube. Pat and I hated the idea of a G-tube; this would become our Alamo, and the doctors did not force us to have the procedure done. With all that Cal would lose that summer—the ability to walk, talk, sit up on her own, feed herself, and use the potty—her needing a feeding tube was the most painful for us, and we assumed, falsely, that it meant we had failed. Looking back, we would come to realize what a mistake this was. It would have been better for Cal and us if we had just gotten the feeding tube right away, so she could take her medications and get the nutrition and fluids she needed. Pat and I had never been around a child who needed a feeding tube, and more so than the other changes, this felt overwhelming to us. So while the doctors marveled at our ability to keep Cal healthy without a tube, we finally got her one.

It was strange, but one of the things that upset me most about MLD was the fact that the tightness in Cal's muscles made her toes point out like she was a ballet dancer, so she could no longer wear shoes. Her scuffed sandals and worn sneakers made me ache when I saw them. Pat tried to give them away because they upset me so much, but I could not stand the idea of parting with them. I had given away the toys and the bike, but somehow the scuffed shoes could not be discarded. The last pair of shoes Cal could wear were more cherished than her first pair. The sight of them could induce the sort of cleansing weeping that purged my body of toxic grief. The shoes are still in my bedroom drawer; I take them out on the anniversary of Cal's diagnosis to time-travel and visit my old life when she could run and play and hug me and hold my hand and kiss me back and say "Daddy."

In those weeks after Cal's diagnosis I also realized how dangerous these visits to the past can be. You can lose yourself in the grief over what's been lost. I tell this to newly diagnosed families all the time, warning them that visits to your old life must be brief. The same thing can be said about contemplating the future; you can become immobilized with fear if you dwell too much on the ending to your child's story. Living with Cal called us to live with no sense of the past and no thought to the future. Even as the disease stole more and more from her, we had to train ourselves to be grateful for what was possible each day.

Like most MLD families, we would be referred to hospice. This sounds terrifying and initially you don't want to hear the h-word, but what you come to see is that caring for a kid like Cal is not something you should do on your own. And anyone who can help you, anyone who shows up at your door and asks, "What do you need?" is not someone you can afford to turn away.

Most people think hospice is morphine drips and your grandpa dying of cancer. But hospice for children is not about managing end-of-life care like it is for adults. It would include music and art therapy, counseling for the whole family, respite care, and a team of people who could be called upon at any moment to help with anything from a hospitalization to signing a death certificate or arranging for an art therapist to work with a sick child's siblings. With Pat's planned stem cell replacement, we ranked as a high-need family, even among other families with terminally ill children. We were fortunate that Cal's diagnosis had come after the Affordable Care Act became law. It included a program called the concurrent care provision. This meant kids like Cal could receive hospice services at their residence, with free medical supplies and hospice nurses working to keep them at home as much as possible, but also were allowed to receive acute care at the hospital, including the ICU.

Having the hospice nurses come to our house and manage Cal's care with us helped us come to terms with what was happening to her and us. We suddenly had an army of people in our lives who knew how to take care of a kid like Cal without drama. Those who work caring for dying children are the most remarkable sort of people you could imagine. They seem genuinely oblivious to how brave or kind they are. To a person, when you ask them why they do the work they do, they will say, "It is an honor and a privilege" to bear "witness" to children's lives.

Hospice soon became a part of our normal, daily routine, the same way my neighbors on the Main Line might consult with a life coach or work with a personal trainer. Our new best friends would be Cal's nurses and aides. That summer, as Cal's world closed in on us dramatically, we were fortunate to have it opened up by the kind and compassionate people helping us care for her. Years later my daughter Camille wrote her college entrance essay about Cal's nurses. We got them Christmas gifts, celebrated their weddings and birthdays, and hosted them at Christmas and Thanksgiving.

That summer our house grew quiet as Cal did not use words or laugh or sing as much, but it was also busier. Our front door was hardly ever locked as social workers, nurses, and supervisors came and went all day long. At the house was Katie, a young aide who put herself through college by taking night shifts caring for Cal. In a movie she might be the ingénue, tall and sweet and hopelessly romantic. Katie loves to dress Callie in pretty outfits, braid her hair, and paint her nails. When she got married she insisted on having Cal be her flower girl. Cal nearly stole the show from the bride because, much to everyone's amazement, she laughed through the priest's droning homily. Renee is the Prince-obsessed, dreadlocked respiratory therapist who takes weekend shifts and likes to rant about President Trump. Then there is Amina, the quiet, thoughtful aide whose own life had been touched by the tragic death of her mother. Amina always watches enjoys watching *Moana* with Cal. Brandi is the stunning social butterfly with many male suitors who never seems to really date. She loves to travel and goes on exciting vacations to Jamaica, Los Angeles, Las Vegas, and Abu Dhabi.

At the heart of the show is Peggy. Peggy was in her fifties when she started to take care of Cal, but she looks a decade younger. She has obsessive-compulsive disorder, and she harnesses all that perfectionism in her care for Cal. Although nurses are supposed to keep a professional distance, Peggy fell in love with Cal right away. She has no biological children, but Cal is her family. Peggy's devotion to Cal is one of the reasons Cal has beaten the odds. One of Cal's doctors once noted, "If every seriously ill child had a nurse like Peggy, this world would be a better place."

When we are not at the doctor or the pool, Cal spends most of her time in just two rooms in our house, her bedroom and the den. She is most happy in the den. Cal and her throne (our Ethan Allen couch) are the center of all activity—and this is the place where we all gather every night to watch her shows or find out how the day has gone. Among her favorite shows are *Caillou* and the BBC cartoon *Kipper*, and she gets annoyed when people change the channel. The disease is starting to damage her vision, but this does not stop her from loving her shows. Smiles and laughs rule her kingdom. She is a homebody, most comfortable around her people. She was like that before she got sick and still is.

The Medicaid approval came just in time to pay for Cal's rapidly growing list of medications. In only a few months that list expanded to include Prilosec and Gas-X to manage GERD and gas; gabapentin for nerve pain; baclofen for spasms, nerve pain, and seizures; Valium for muscle tone and seizures; Senna to get the gut moving; Keppra for seizures; Culturelle (an over-the-counter probiotic) for digestion; hyoscyamine to reduce stomach cramps; and Miralax and daily enemas and suppositories for constipation. Each day Pat and I begin her care first thing in the morning, and we cannot go to bed until she gets her last medication at midnight. In the corner by Cal's bed is a table filled with her medications; a whiteboard lists the times to administer them and the dosages. Underneath the table with the medications is a go bag with changes of clothes, Cal's medical records, and blankets so that we can go to the hospital in minutes if necessary.

Cal is the sun our lives orbit around. Our house is quieter since she became ill; there are no messes from discarded toys and shoes or abandoned arts and crafts projects. PJ and Camille know they must wash their hands as soon as they get home from school and before they see their sister in her room. They do not have friends over often. When Camille and PJ cough or sneeze or get a fever, before I care for them I remind them to avoid their sister and father because a common cold could result in a hospitalization.

Nurses come and go all day long and they no longer knock; they just let themselves in through the back door and put their lunches in the fridge and go to see Cal and get updated by the last shift. Pat and the kids don't scream and yell the way other families do because there are always other people around. Cal's medical files are stored in three-ring binders and her bedroom closet is filled with catheters, extra buttons for her feeding tube, syringes, and assorted medical devices. Cal does not own a single pair of shoes. Medications and diapers get shipped to the house so frequently that we are on a first-name basis with the FedEx and UPS deliverymen. There is a sign on our front door warning people not to smoke in and around our home because there are oxygen tanks on the premises.

The Make-A-Wish trip to Martha's Vineyard would be our last family holiday with Pat and me and all three of the children together. Pat and I have left the state together only three times since then, once to go to my uncle's funeral in New Jersey, once on a day trip to see Glenda Jackson perform *King*

Lear on Broadway, and the other time to testify to the FDA. Either Pat or I is always within half an hour of the house in case Cal needs to be admitted, and our fire department has our name on a list in case she needs to be transported by ambulance or the paramedics have to resuscitate her if she codes.

BURNING UP ON REENTRY

Pat's father was dying from pancreatic cancer, and his mother was sick and frail and overwhelmed. But Pat's instinct to protect them came at a high price: pretending things were fine when they most definitely were not. Hiding Cal's illness from my in-laws was possible only because they lived in Ireland, an ocean away.

It astounded me that my husband would deny himself the most basic form of love and comfort from his own family so as not to burden them. With my parents in Boston, it seemed impossible for me to lie to them. Not that I had an impulse to protect them; instead, it seemed to me I desperately needed them to survive all of it. But looking back I wish I had not told my dad about Cal. Of all the things he had faced in his life, her illness devastated him in a way I had not fully anticipated.

My father and I fought, initially because he was angry at me "for believing the doctors" and "accepting their prognosis." Though my father was an engineer and a firm believer in math and physics, his faith in God and miracles trumped all of that. He was an unwavering optimist; he had come to America with nothing and earned a college degree and made a fortune in Boston's booming real estate market.

Dad believed in miracles because he was one. He was born in 1940 in Greece on the island of Chios during the Nazi occupation. As an infant he had had a blockage in his urethra, a condition that should have killed him. Surgery even in a state-of-the-art hospital in the United States would have come with risks, but on an island in the Aegean Sea in the middle of a battle zone, the doctor told his mother and grandmother that my father's death was inevitable. The story my father told was that his grandmother, refusing to accept the diagnosis, had traveled to the holiest shrine in Greece and found a monk who managed to perform the procedure with great success. Though my father suffered from chronic infections and would have surgeries throughout the rest of his life, his doctors at Mass General marveled that he had survived childhood. They had even written papers about him.

My father wanted me to be like my great-grandmother and take Cal to Greece and see the monks and pray for a miracle. To my father that made more sense than listening to the doctors. When I tried to explain that the damage to Cal's brain and central nervous system had started years ago and could not be slowed or reversed, that the MRIs were irrefutable evidence, he became enraged, and I would have to hang up the phone.

September meant going back to school, not only for Camille and PJ but also for Pat and me. Pat had declared that he would take no time off from work even as he prepared for the scheduled stem cell replacement in December. A stem cell replacement would use high-dose chemotherapy to wipe out cancer-ridden hematopoietic stem cells—or the mother cells that produce blood—and reboot his body with his own stem cells that had been cleared of the cancer. The treatment was not a cure, but it could get Pat years of a remissive state with the help of daily maintenance chemotherapy. If the stem-cell-replacement procedure worked he wouldn't need to do the weekly infusions and would see the doctor every three months.

For Pat, cancer was an inconvenience, keeping him from fulfilling his duties as a breadwinner, father, and husband. He didn't want to take a medical leave from work and had scheduled the procedure for after exams. He didn't want a pay cut when Cal was sick. The idea of returning to work weeks after a stem cell replacement was ambitious, if not demented, as far as I was concerned. But Pat is a freight train; he would not stop.

Our friend Susan supported his decision. Two years earlier, at age forty, she had undergone a double mastectomy and had managed to return to class after just one week. When she was on bed rest she insisted on hosting the students at her home for the lectures she could not stand up to give on campus. Susan believed in the healing power of work, and she defended Pat when I said they were both crazy and needed to rest. Susan was the sort of cancer patient who joked about how breast cancer meant her boobs would now be enviably perky and make her look great in a swimsuit when other women her age had to wear industrial-strength bras.

A typical stem-cell-replacement patient could be in the hospital for a month. When Pat asked his doctors at Penn to tell him what the shortest possible stay was, they said his body would tell them when he could be discharged. Because the treatment rebooted his immune system, he would go home only when his blood cell counts were at the levels that showed he could fight off infection once he left the hospital. But Pat wanted a number. A nurse recalled a patient who had managed to be discharged after fifteen days. "But that was the exception, not the rule," she added, and "besides, he was very young, just twenty years old." Pat became fixated on the number, determined to get home in time to spend Christmas with the kids. He would not break the record, but he only lost by a day. True to his word, Pat walked off the transplant floor in time to be home for Cal's birthday and Christmas. In three months Dr. Hartner would declare that the transplant had worked; Pat never seemed to doubt that he would be okay. "The world owed us a win," he said. The news that Pat's cancer was in a remissive state gave us a reprieve for the first time in a year.

Not all multiple myeloma patients go into remission after a stem cell replacement; many are not so fortunate. Dr. Hartner had tried to prepare us for a poor outcome, warning me that Pat might need a second transplant if the first one failed. After hearing the news that he was in remission, Pat wrote an open letter on my Facebook page (since he hates social media and has no account of his own) thanking our friends and family for the months of support. It would be one of the only times he would share his emotions publicly with the people who cared for him. "I am a fighter," Pat would tell me. He did not mean that in the offhand way people talked about "fighting" cancer. This was a sacred pledge to me and the children. The cancer might win in the end, but Pat needed us to understand that he would never make it easy.

Going back to work in the fall to start teaching after Cal's diagnosis made me feel like a space capsule burning up on re-entry. The summer had been Make-A-Wish and doctors' visits and eating Oreos at the pool. The idea of getting in front of a classroom to teach college kids terrified me. In the weeks and months after Cal's and Pat's diagnoses, hearing mundane questions like "How was your summer?" and "How are your kids?" was like getting beaten over the head with a baseball bat. Sometimes people asked such questions the way you do in casual conversation because they "had not heard the news." Explaining Cal's diagnosis to friends and families and well-meaning strangers was continually traumatizing. I had to answer questions about the worst thing that had ever happened to me over and over again.

Even with people who "knew," I had to decide whether to provide the sanitized version or actually tell the truth. It did not take long to figure out that when people asked about Cal, Pat, my father-in-law, and my dad, they really did not want to hear about our meeting with the oncologist and the fact that my father used a bag to collect urine or that Cal's disease was more advanced than the doctors first guessed and we were now getting referred to hospice. People wanted to hear I was okay and managing. Most did not want the truth of the nervous breakdown or the crying in the shower or my gaining twenty pounds in twelve weeks.

Right after Cal got sick, I lacked the discipline to tell a more socially palatable version of the truth. The rage and grief needed to go someplace, and I lived by a standard of unfiltered truth. When a colleague told me I looked good, I called out her obvious if well-meaning lie, pointing out that I was wearing the clothes I had slept in, had not combed my hair, and had gone up a dress size. If I wanted people to feel as bad as I did, I found all I needed to do was tell them how things were. There was a thrilling power to be felt in seeing people recoil in horror when I told them of my routine of doctors and specialists and infusions for my husband and my dad or recounted how Cal had uttered her final word.

My appearance was increasingly akin to bag-lady chic. That summer I had gone through my closet and thrown out most of the clothes that no longer fit. Pat said nothing when I declared I would never need makeup or high heels again since there was no reason to be pretty or put-together. I loaded up the car with the clothes I wore in my old life when I gave lectures and traveled to conferences and wrote books. The suit from Nordstrom I had purchased for a keynote in Washington, DC, and the slacks I had worn for the lecture at Harvard were dumped in contractor bags and donated to Goodwill.

On the Main Line, where the appearance of perfect kids, perfect marriages, and perfect careers is prized, some people started to avoid us. When I was in the supermarket or encountered neighbors, they might ignore my gaze. After all, while standing in the Whole Foods checkout line I might talk about how my kid needed a feeding tube or might discuss the latest battle with Medicaid. That made us a horrifying reminder of how the carefully manicured lawns and ageless, elegant women driving Range Rovers could be struck down by tragedy at any moment.

On a good day I could perform the socially acceptable response of thanking people for their concern and lying about how we were managing. But there were some days when I felt compelled to tell the truth. I would go through the blow-by-blow of how Cal was now paralyzed, and we had been referred to hospice care, and how Pat was going to be admitted to Penn for a stem cell replacement. We could talk about how my father's cancer left my brilliant, funny dad bedridden and housebound, and that my father-in-law's inoperable pancreatic cancer meant his life was near the end.

At work, when my colleagues met to discuss the mundane issues of budgets and enrollments, I greeted the agenda items with an unrestrained id. I declared that the meetings were a profound waste of time because we had been writing the same mission statement or reviewing the same proposals for how to address diversity for a decade. It was thrilling and liberating to be unmoored from the social conventions that had trapped me in my previous life. As a college professor, the flexibility of my job, combined with my tolerance for eccentricity and bad behavior, protected me. Without tenure—or if I had had a real job at Wal-Mart or a law firm—such behavior might have gotten me fired.

My emotional reactions were short-circuited. My grief over Pat, Cal, and my father robbed me of the ability to process feelings the way normal people do. I would watch movies featuring tragedy and heartbreak, but the Hollywood versions of ICUs and doctors giving patients the news that they were dying were pale versions of my real life. One night, finding Erich Segal's *Love Story* on cable, I was struck by what a whiny pussy Ryan O'Neal's Oliver was. I envied the people whose kids had cancer in the St. Jude's ads. Only 20 percent of children with pediatric cancer die, so what were they complaining about? I even penned an essay (thankfully left unpublished) titled "Why I Am Jealous of Parents Whose Kids Have Brain Tumors."

The Sandy Hook school shooting was different. The day of the shooting, my students asked my opinion about the tragedy. The criminology and sociological literature on mass shootings and gun violence had long been the focus of my introductory courses. But now that I was the parent of a dying child, I could not get past the terrible connection I shared with the Sandy Hook parents. I was moving in slow motion, imagining the horror these families were coming to terms with.

For all of 2012 we were in crisis mode, reeling from one unimaginable situation to another. There were days when I would drop Cal off for her occupational therapy, go across the street to see Pat, who was getting an infusion at Penn's Abramson Center, then go home to order a pizza for the kids, and later head out to teach and read papers. Looking back, I have no idea how I survived that year. It is amazing to realize that you can endure catastrophes just because the momentum of everyday life pushes you forward. It has precious little to do with intentionality and bravery and far more to do with physics.

My father-in-law, father, and Cal were referred to hospice within months of one another that year. We lost my father-in-law, Paddy, in September 2012. As he succumbed to pancreatic cancer and his body went into system failure, a massive stroke would claim him on Yom Kippur. Pat had to get permission from his oncologist to make the trip to Ireland to attend the funeral. I could not attend the service to say goodbye to the wonderful and charming man who had been so happy that I had made his only son a husband and father.

My father-in-law's death came quickly. His medical team in Ireland had decided to focus on palliative care right at the time of diagnosis, and he died soon thereafter. My father's death highlighted the differences in the American and European systems. Dad would spend months undergoing treatment at Mass General, where the doctors sought to make the cancer behave itself. But not long after Cal's diagnosis, he lost his focus and optimism. He stopped believing in miracles; to me it seemed he could not bear to face a world where he got to live and Cal did not. Despite the risks, his medical team at Mass General had elected to perform an emergency surgery to remove a section of his bowel. Dad now had a bag collecting urine and stool in contraptions strapped to the side of his leg. The man who loved to eat could hardly be tempted to take a bite from a doughnut. More and more, he was disoriented and confused.

I felt abandoned and betrayed because the celebrated progress in medical science could not save the people I loved. The medical-industrial complex's promises of using technology and breakthroughs to defeat disease and bring about miracles were bait-and-switch marketing. During my father's final hospitalization there was a full-court press from his medical team for him to sign a Do Not Resuscitate form, but he refused, telling the doctors, "What's the big rush? If I code, why don't you take a day or two, pray, and figure out the next move." I got home to Boston in time to help sign him out of active treatment and enroll him in hospice. My elementary school friend Amy Khazham, who was now a hospice nurse, picked me up from the airport and came with me to talk to my dad. She had not seen him or me in more than thirty years, but she had heard about Cal and rushed to help.

As wonderful and generous as my father was, hospitals and sickness terrified him. He had not even gone to his own parents' burial, and he never took us to visit their graves. My father's guilt over not being the kind of man to run to our side when Cal got sick was suffocating him. I tried to assure him that there was nothing for me to forgive; his anguish over not seeing Cal was causing him as much pain as the cancer.

So many people I thought were our friends had not been able to face Cal's illness, and I preferred not to see the people who could not see beyond her disease. The truth was it was liberating to declutter our lives of people who were not brave and loyal. My father was different, I cannot lie, and his absence had been wounding. But I also found it nearly impossible to remain angry at this man I loved so much and saw so clearly.

Even in his weakened state Dad found me transformed. My father adored his children but also possessed a clear-eyed view of their limits. As a kid I had been prone to sadness and the kind of self-indulgent bouts of depression that are possible only when you don't have any real troubles. Dad knew I was clever, possessing above-average intelligence, but I could be flighty, selfish, and prone to panicking. When he saw me speaking to nurses and doctors and spending hours in the hospital with him, he noticed the metamorphosis.

"Mariamou," he said one day as I visited with him in rehab. I was startled by the use of his pet name for me—"my Maria"—which he hadn't done since I was a little girl. "When did you become like this?" He was struck by how good I was in a crisis, how his illness did not frighten or overwhelm me. He was amazed that I could be so brave. I said, "Daddy, you taught me."

He shook his head. "No, I didn't."

We lost my father on December 27, 2013, four years and two days after we brought Cal home from the hospital and the day after his forty-eighth wedding anniversary.

That year the hospice nurses caring for my father and Cal taught me everything about how to live. While most medical professionals spend all their energies focused on learning the skills and mastering the science that will allow them to make sickness and death behave, hospice nurses focus on a sort of medicine that puts patients at the center of their own care and rejects other medical professionals' insistence that death can be defeated.

The nurses who care for dying children showed us how to make room for the joy and the beauty of what was possible in Cal's life. So many people who learned of her diagnosis were so frightened for us and for her that it was impossible for them to move beyond the sadness and grief of it all. Even the doctors at CHOP who treated dying children were not much better prepared than Pat or me to accept how Cal's story would end. We were a reminder of the limits of medicine, the cruelty and randomness of sickness, and of how even good parents who did everything right could not protect their children.

The doctors at CHOP and the team from our pediatric hospice program recognized that Cal was beautiful and filled with love. She was perfect because she could only give love and receive it and was incapable of cruelty, meanness, or selfishness. When you ask these men and women why they do this work, caring for children who do not grow up, they will tell you, to a person, that they are called to do it. One doctor acquaintance, not realizing I had a terminally ill child, said that the doctors who were in hospice or palliative care were burned-out oncologists. It was true, CHOP's palliative care team had come from the oncology world, but they were not discouraged or hopeless; far from it. Among all the doctors and nurses we came to know, the palliative care and hospice teams were the ones we relied on the most. They could see that death was not the worst thing we faced. So many of their peers, brilliant doctors who devoted years of their life to medical school and residencies and fellowships, had not fully come to terms with the fact that their patients, even children, would die.

Cal was making me into a person whom no one recognized, not even my dad. That's when I came to realize that when the worst thing happens, you become brave because you have nothing left to be afraid of and you realize you are superhuman. The things that make mere mortals shudder are your everyday reality, and when you run out of things to be afraid of, you find that nothing can stop you. We could not conquer MLD, but love (Cal's love for us and ours for her) was indestructible. MLD could not touch it. With this truth I abandoned the idea I had control of anything; that realization was liberating. Embarrassment, vanity, insecurity—forces that limited ordinary people—no longer touched me. I was not brave so much as unfettered by those anxieties and fears. In these flashes of clarity (or madness), it seemed to me grief had made me extraordinary. Cal was making all of us extraordinary.

But on the bad days it was impossible to deny that the MLD was defeating us—decisively—on all the other fronts. We worried about whether Cal would live for the three years that some of the doctors had told us about. Dr. Waldman had told us the disease would plateau or stabilize, but Pat and I saw little evidence of that during the summer of 2012.

By then, Pat and I were making plans for Cal's funeral, and we debated the pros and cons of cremation over burial. I thought about bringing her ashes back to the sea on Martha's Vineyard, but then we worried about not being able to visit when we needed to be close to her. The idea of letting her be swept out to sea was beautiful and lyrical, but, selfishly, I thought I could not let her go. Pat and I both wanted to keep her close. Other leukodystrophy families had elaborate headstones or kept their children's ashes in a place of honor in their home. My new friends were the parents of dying children, and instead of saving for college we planned funerals and chose headstones and thought about the perfect outfit to bury our children in.

Telling my children that their father, both grandfathers, and sister were all sick and proximate to death required a whole new way of communicating. I spent days trying to decide how much I would tell them. Would I give them the names of Cal's and their father's diseases? In the age of Google and the internet, I worried they would look them up and learn terrifying things. That first year I still clung to the notion that I could protect Camille and PJ and even myself from the trauma and pain of it all. I kept wanting to promise them we would be okay—that their father and sister and all of us would be okay. But that was not true. My tough-love message to Cal's brother and sister was that they were not allowed to complain because Cal never did. There would be no time for self-pity or regrets, for they are pointless pursuits.

Throughout the summer, during our many conversations with Camille and PJ about their sister, father, and grandfathers, I focused on how much they were loved, stressing that illness and death could not change that. As their mom I might not be able to change what was happening, but I could control the fact that it was not their job to take care of me; rather it was my job to take care of them. Their father and I wanted them to have a life of joy and happiness, and while we couldn't cure Cal of her disease, we could control how much we let disease define how we lived our lives.

Camille and PJ were allowed to be angry—furious at this disease for devastating their lives—and they were. They could also be angry with me for not being the mother they deserved or that I wanted to be for them. They denied being upset with me, though they could not help but blame me. Still, they would grow protective of me when I took responsibility for how their lives had been forever changed by illness.

I apologized that my time at the hospital meant the house would be messier and that I would not be as involved with their lives. But I told them that no matter what happened, they should never doubt my love for them, and that I would do everything in my power to protect them as much as I could from everything that I had control over.

I shared that they were allowed to be afraid as well. While I didn't dwell on it with them, I told them I was scared too. But while fear was intense and overwhelming, our superpowers to defeat it were hope and love and gratitude for the things that no disease, no trauma, and even no death could take away.

How careful the kids were with me; they had learned to be stoic, too, holding in their feelings tightly so as not to burden their father or me.

It is fortunate that even though I struggled mightily at work, the best advice I have ever received, the insight that helped me change and find a way forward, came from a Jesuit priest named Peter Clark, the head of SJU's bioethics program. He had worked in Haiti and advocated for the nation's first safe-injection site, in Philadelphia, to manage the city's overdose epidemic. Back in 2012, he worked at St. Christopher's Hospital, a children's hospital that served the city's poorer residents. He provided ethical consultations in the pediatric ICU, advising doctors and patient families on caring for babies who had been born too early and with maladies that science sometimes lacked the language to understand.

I was back at work but barely functioning when a colleague told me to see Peter. He had a reputation for being demanding and exacting and even a bit arrogant, not the sort of avuncular priest one imagines would work at a children's hospital. But the day I went to see him it was clear that he had spent a lot of time talking to parents like me. Peter seemed unfazed by emotional distress and suffering. I told him about how I believed Cal was turning into a mermaid and I dreamed of dying with her. Peter absorbed my words without alarm or judgment. I was the mother of a dying child; he understood women like me, and he was not afraid of my ravings.

Peter would then go on to say the wisest and truest thing that anyone has ever said to me. All these years later it is something I tell all the parents I meet when they find out their children have leukodystrophy. It is the only thing anyone said to me in those terrible months that offered any real comfort.

I confessed how scared I was: "I don't think I can face this."

He took a deep breath and said, "If you have the courage to be around children like your daughter, children who are dying, they will teach you the very meaning of life. I promise."

Could this be true? It was undeniable that the grief of the past year since Pat, our fathers, and Cal had become ill had changed me. Increasingly, what I had assumed to be a nervous breakdown was giving way to an intense clarity. Loving Cal had given us laser-like focus on the perfection and magic of what is possible. There had to be meaning in all of it; Cal's story was too beautiful and heartbreaking to belong only to our family. How could we share what she was teaching us with others? After all, when your child does not get to grow up, their legacy is the only thing you'll have. In the end you are not remembered for what you do or say but how you make people feel. And the way Cal made us feel was miraculous. More and more, I longed to share it with others.

LEMONADE

Not everyone has the capacity to transform pain into action. To be sure, not everyone who suffers loss should feel obligated to start raising a million dollars or climb Mount Everest. But for those who are in search of solace, harnessing pain to help others is a salve. The Greeks have a word for this, *agape*, the sort of love that becomes a force for change in the world. After meeting Dr. Waldman and Father Peter, I was slowly awakening to the idea that Cal's story was powerful and her life had meaning beyond our family.

It was not difficult to find inspiring role models. There were the Sandy Hook parents who had fought for gun-control legislation. The reason the number of drunk-driving deaths had fallen by nearly 46 percent since the 1990s was the tireless efforts of Candy Lightner, whose thirteen-year-old daughter, Cari, was killed by a drunk driver in 1980. That tragedy led to the creation of Mothers Against Drunk Driving (MADD). There was the mother of Michael Brown, Lesley McSpadden, who ran for city council in Ferguson, Missouri, to heal her community and became a voice for the Black Lives Matter movement. Living on Philadelphia's Main Line, we were fortunate to have a remarkable role model in our neighbor Alex Scott, the little girl who literally turned lemons into lemonade to find a cure for cancer even when doctors would not be able to save her.

If you have ever purchased Country Time Lemonade or watched *Oprah*, you have probably heard of Alex Scott. In 1996, at the age of one, she was diagnosed with neuroblastoma, a rare form of pediatric cancer. At the time there were precious few treatment options. Even though Alex underwent a stem cell transplant, the doctors told her parents, Liz and Jay, that there was little they could do. But the Scotts are fighters, and they relocated from Connecticut to Pennsylvania so Alex could be close to one of the few teams of doctors working on treatments for neuroblastoma. The team at "Alex's hospital" was at CHOP, where Cal had been diagnosed. For the rest of Alex's life, scans, infusions, central lines, and clinical trials would become routine. Her older brother, Patrick, and her parents could barely remember life before cancer.

Children who face life-limiting conditions are extraordinary for a host of reasons, and yet what they long for most is the normal and unexceptional. While healthy kids will bring in a note from their doctor if they have a scratchy throat or stomach cramps, a young person with cancer views it as a defeat and a disappointment when they cannot be in class. As a professor I have taught students dealing with cancer and cystic fibrosis and have been struck by how they fight mightily against missing a day of school or calling out sick. Alex Scott was no different; she adored being at school and cherished the days when she was well enough to pretend to be like other children.

It was after one of her frequent hospital admissions that four-year-old Alex announced to her parents, "When I get out of the hospital I want to do a lemonade stand to raise money to help kids with cancer." True to her word, after Alex was discharged from the hospital and a day after her fourth birthday, she hosted her first lemonade stand and raised two thousand dollars. Her brother Patrick helped.

Alex continued to host the stands every year, often around her birthday. Birthdays are surreal when you are sick. For most youngsters, birthdays are exciting—all about looking forward to another year—but when death looms on the horizon, birthdays are reminders of a clock that is ticking. And when Alex turned eight, her doctors understood that they were running out of options to stop the cancer.

In 2004, which would be the last year of her life, Alex announced that her lemonade stand was going to raise a million dollars for cancer research. She informed her doctors and parents that the money would not go toward saving her life but toward finding cures for the other kids with different kinds of cancers living the life she had. She wanted to help the kids who came after her.

Knowing what I know now about children who live in such close proximity to death, I believe that Alex saw it as less of an intruder and more of a companion. Besides, because Alex could not imagine the life she was supposed to lead with the clarity her parents could, her ache for that alternative existence was not so crippling. For Alex, cancer was always there. I understand this because this is how Cal is. My Cal cannot mourn the life her father and I dreamed for her because she has no sense of what that might be. Her world is our family, and she has found a way to mine her life and this tiny world for every bit of joy and happiness that is possible for her.

So even as Alex and her parents understood time was running out, rather than taking a trip to Hawaii or heading to Disney World, Alex chose to invest in miracles for other children. She clung to the joy of the normal, or whatever approximation can be manufactured when an eight-year-old knows she is going to die. Could it be that Alex started her lemonade stands around her birthday celebrations so her parents would have a way to celebrate her life after she was gone? Was it her gift to her parents, who would need a way to fill their life with meaning and purpose? Is it possible that a four-year-old figured out that suffering was a force for changing the world? Could it be that she taught this truth to her grieving and devastated parents?

Alex would accomplish a lifetime of goals by the time she died on August 1, 2004, at the age of eight. She had appeared on *Oprah* and the *Today* show, raised more than a million dollars for cancer research, and started a charity. Alex's Lemonade Stand Foundation had funded breakthroughs that would double the survivorship rate for neuroblastoma patients and provide for the first CAR T-cell treatment to be approved by the FDA for pediatric lymphoma patients. Twenty years after doctors told Liz and Jay Scott that Alex would not get to grow up, the family is still carrying on their daughter's mission. And Alex's older brother, Patrick, a Harvard graduate, recently joined the foundation he helped start as a little boy twenty years ago. To date, Alex's Lemonade Stand Foundation has raised a staggering $175 million.

One drizzly spring day in 2012, just weeks before I would come to realize how much Liz Scott and I and our two little girls shared in common, I had taken PJ and Cal to the Alex's Lemonade Stand Foundation Carnival at the Penn Wynne School. If she had lived, Alex would have been sixteen. PJ had nagged me to go, having heard the story of Alex and the lemonade stand at school and probably because he wanted to win prizes and eat pizza. Cal was still able to run and play, and though I did not think she was seriously ill, her gait issues and lack of speech were starting to trouble us.

Alex's Lemonade Stand Carnival is a festival of games, raffles, pizza, and hot dogs. The only reason you would not think it was a regular elementary school field day were the pictures in the program of the little girl whose hair is falling out in patches because of her cancer treatments. The program also features the Scott family sharing memories, telling the story of Alex and the lemonade stand, and welcoming families with children who are undergoing treatment. It is a day when no one stares at the kids who have central lines and are bald from chemotherapy and radiation. Rather than being avoided, they are embraced and showered with love and attention.

On the stage near the school building, even as Cal and I played in the field far from the stage, I could see Liz Scott. Surrounded by photographs of the little girl who had been gone for so many years now, she was giving a speech about childhood cancer research. Patrick, who was a senior in high school and would be heading off to college in the fall, gave a touching speech about his younger sister and the birthday that had led to the original lemonade stands.

Liz and Jay spoke about all the money they had raised and the research that Alex's efforts had made possible. That day, even though I had no sense of how much our lives would change in the next few weeks, I wondered how Liz and Jay Scott felt about the paradox of Alex's illness and death making it possible for so many other children to be saved. Did they take comfort and find peace in that calculus or did it fill them with rage? I wondered how they made sense of sharing their daughter with the world and grieving so publicly in order to raise money and push research. It seemed to me that Alex was not really even gone; her photos and spirit were everywhere.

And what did it mean for Liz and Jay's three boys? How could you be the brother to a heroine who captivated the world, a little girl who had been interviewed by Oprah? How could the Scotts surround themselves with the pain and suffering of other families and relive the very same anguish that had stolen their only daughter? For many people, once their cancer treatment is finished, they never want to return to the hospital. Here was a family that had immersed themselves completely in the world that had taken their daughter and sister from them. Was this courage or pure insanity? Did doing these amazing things allow them to live with their ghosts and grief in a public, socially acceptable way? I thought to myself, "I could never be so brave."

As I stood there watching Cal in her lovely yellow dress chasing after her brother, I wondered whether tragedy befalls certain families so they can make miracles possible for other people. Was this suffering part of some divine plan to make the world better? Because I didn't know how similar Liz Scott and I actually were, I watched Cal and PJ eat pizza and play and reminded myself that in spite of how hard things were with Pat, I must be grateful for the gift of my healthy children.

Liz would reenter my life that August, just four months after Cal attended the lemonade stand event, a month after she was diagnosed. The idea of speaking to Liz had come to me on my nighttime walks through the neighborhood. Meeting a mother who had buried a child would give me a chance to understand how to endure after the worst thing that could happen happens.

I turned to my friend Marissa, who knew I was struggling. We're both professors as well as practical problem-solvers, and we had nicknamed Marissa the mayor of our town because she seemed to know everyone, from the police chief to the wife of the coach of the Philadelphia 76ers. I knew Marissa would be able to arrange for Liz and me to connect, and she did. I now had Liz Scott's direct phone number and an official introduction from a trusted mutual friend. We arranged to speak the next afternoon.

When I phoned at our prearranged time, Liz picked up on the first ring. Clearly she had been waiting for me. Liz's voice immediately makes people feel better. Despite her extraordinary life and great personal tragedy, she excels at appearing normal. I envied this ability to impersonate regular people who had not lost a child. It was hard to imagine her ever being like me, crying in the shower, eating her weight in Oreos every night, and never combing her hair. But while she may not have grieved her daughter the same way I was grieving Cal, I guessed that this appearance of normalcy that was so reassuring so soon after Cal's diagnosis was a veneer, something she had spent years carefully crafting for herself. At the time, my greatest fear was that if I truly loved my daughter, I needed to submerge myself in grief. I worried that I would become the kind of lady who mutters to herself in the supermarket parking lot and spends her afternoons drinking coffee by herself at Starbucks, and is found dead in her house alone, surrounded by her dogs and old newspapers. I hoped that in Liz Scott I had discovered a role model and a path forward.

Liz was the first person I met after Cal's diagnosis who did not seem frightened or overwhelmed by my emotions and fears or by the questions I wanted to ask. "The grief is so crippling and overwhelming," I said. "How did you manage the pain of it all?" Liz reassured me that the devastating, immobilizing pain I felt in the weeks after hearing Cal's diagnosis would become a more manageable, chronic ailment. She continued, "It took me until two years after Alex's death to feel something like my old self. It's like the grief just builds up in you, and every month or so it becomes so much I need to cry to get it out or else I cannot function." It felt like a judge had given me a prison sentence: two years to feel like myself again after Cal's diagnosis and then two years after she had died to put myself together again.

I had learned from the social workers at CHOP, who had explained that I was in a state of anticipatory grief. It was as if my brain realized I was about to crash a car and was preparing me for the impact. That is actually what causes whiplash: you tighten your muscles, and the pain results from the strain of your tensed-up body absorbing the force of the blow. That is what anticipatory grief is like.

My next question was about how she dealt with Alex's brothers. Camille and PJ could see their sister was sick and knew she had been in the hospital, but we still had not found the courage to tell them about Cal's disease. My denial was powerful; I refused to say the disease's name or even Google it to learn more.

Liz shared that she had always taken a "need-to-know" approach with her children. She did not elaborate on this, but I took it to mean that she would give her children bad news only when it was impossible to protect them from what was happening. She and Jay had not burdened their kids with all the excruciating details of Alex's treatment and illness. Liz told me it was their oldest son, Patrick, who had the strongest ties to their family's life before cancer. He had hosted the original lemonade stand with his sister and possessed the most fully formed memories of Alex's life and death. Alex's younger brothers were born after her diagnosis and were very young when she died. Their emotional connection to Alex was sustained by their parents' memories and work in her name.

Liz told me that Alex's illness and death made it difficult to become annoyed with her other children. Other parents would get upset about a bad grade or a messy room, but such things did not trouble Liz. Part of this may have been the exhaustion of caring for a child who would die. But more than that, Alex had taught Liz to be grateful for the gift of healthy children. The fact that her kids were healthy meant they could roll their eyes at her or forget to fold the laundry. These were gifts to be cherished. It was difficult to stop being grateful for the fact that her children were there to drive her nuts. Besides, when her sons acted like other kids from the Main Line, she allowed herself to think that maybe the tragedy and trauma of Alex's death had not totally ruined their claim to "ordinary" childhoods.

I wanted Liz to explain to me how, the day after she buried her only daughter, she had not fled from the hospitals and all mention of cancer and research and neuroblastomas. In the decades since a doctor had told her that her eighteen-month-old child would die, why had she had immersed herself in the world that had destroyed her comfortable life and the blissful assumption that children outlive their parents? She now devoted her life, full time, 24/7, to the thing that had brought so much suffering and pain and ruin. The thing that had taken her little girl. This amazed me most of all.

It was at this point in the conversation that it seemed Liz would reveal the pain that she was so compassionately keeping from me that day. She was talking about Alex and what she missed most about her daughter. Liz said, "I would give anything to have a sixteen-year-old girl in my house, driving us crazy." The very things her friends complained about were just what she ached to have.

Laughing, Liz regained her composure, careful not to burden me with her grief. "This is not the life I ever would have chosen for myself," she said. "I never intended to be an expert on pediatric cancer and cancer research, but Alex got me here, and I can see this was something I am meant to do. After all, as a friend once told me, normal people don't get to change the world."

I wanted to know how she could share Alex with the rest of the world and revisit the pain and grief of losing her over and over again. Liz acknowledged, "The truth is, I don't share everything with the people. There are parts of Alex that I keep just for myself."

My last question had been tormenting me, keeping me awake at night for weeks, a question I had dared not ask anyone for fear they would insist on immediately accompanying me to the hospital. The truth was that thoughts of killing myself and Cal were always there, lurking in the background. Though confident I would never act on them, there was a part of me that had to consider suicide as a rational strategy for dealing with this nightmare. But there was something about Liz that made me trust her—that made me recognize that she wasn't afraid of the things that scared normal people who did not know the pain she and I felt. I sensed that even if Liz had never contemplated ending her own life, she surely knew what it felt like to long to die to be with your baby. I also understood that like me, she had died the day she heard the doctors tell her Alex would die. Grief had made us the walking dead, moving forward through the ruins of our old lives.

I asked Liz about how she had buried her child. I won't share more of what we discussed; it is too intimate, too painful to repeat unless you must plan a child's funeral, and I would never violate Liz's privacy. But she said one thing I can share: "Be sure you have some place close to go, so you can go and be close or feel close to your child when you need to see them." After nearly two hours, I had to let this inspirational woman go. I wanted to go live with her. Here was the first person who made me feel that I could be brave. Her generosity that August day probably saved my life. Even though it would take me more time to understand fully what Liz and Alex could teach our family, there was no denying this conversation offered a way forward. Liz and I still see each other every few months, going out for coffee or lunch and fighting over who gets to pay the bill. These days, as I have gotten better at impersonating a normal woman, sometimes she grants me the privilege of sharing her burdens or worries. It is an honor to offer support to Liz Scott and a compliment that she now sees I am strong enough to share my advice and teach her anything.

Before she got off the phone that day, Liz left me with one final question: Why had I given up hope? "There must be some research you can support," she suggested. "I'm sure they can use your help—you could start to fundraise." I was touched that Liz believed I had the capacity to be so selfless and brave.

But I did tell Liz what I knew. That there was a gene therapy clinical trial in Milan that seemed like science fiction. That doctors said the therapy might be available in another ten or twenty years. That it would never help Cal. That we were not even granted a chance to fight for her life. It was painful to be reminded that pediatric cancer research was in far better shape than the work being done to address Cal's orphaned disease.

CUPCAKES

My son PJ likes to say he came up with the idea to sell cupcakes, which is mostly true. For the sake of full disclosure, PJ stole the idea from Alex's Lemonade Stand, though, to be sure, it was more homage than theft. The same part of PJ's brain that makes it possible for him to believe in Santa and the Easter Bunny allowed this lively, loving brother, who was seven when his sister was diagnosed with leukodystrophy, to believe we could find a cure for Cal's disease by hosting bake sales. PJ's goal was to sell a million cupcakes to raise a million dollars. When a local journalist asked why he had chosen this goal, he answered, "One million was just the largest number I could imagine when I was little."

We started selling cupcakes in the winter of 2013 as we braced ourselves for the first anniversary of Cal's diagnosis and tried to celebrate Cal's birthday. Some of those early events were so utterly disastrous it's not clear to anyone why we continued.

For years Pat and I had purchased cakes for special occasions at the Ultimate Bake Shoppe, a local bakery, including a particularly spectacular carrot cake for Pat's fortieth birthday party. Joanne, the bakery's owner, had become a part of our family, and she loved to give Cal treats from behind the counter. She had seen me soon after we learned that Cal had MLD, and I had told her the whole story.

Speaking to shopkeepers about Cal was easier than talking to my own family, just as you unload to people on a plane rather than your supposed best friends. Joanne adopted me, which worked out well since nice Italian ladies share a great deal in common with Greek ladies when it comes to their crisis-management style. To this day, when Joanne is working in the bakery she directs the girls behind the counter not to take my money and usually forces a bag of muffins, cookies, or scones on me. Encountering Joanne was akin to a drug addict running into her dealer; when I was clean, I would try to avoid her. But on the days I needed a fix, she would be the first person I would seek out, heading to her bakery when I'd told Pat I was going grocery shopping, purportedly to buy fish and vegetables. As soon as Joanne heard about PJ's cupcake idea, she was in and without any hesitation said she would provide cupcakes for our first fundraiser. Everyone who had offered help was grateful for the chance to do something more than watch as Cal grew sicker.

For the doomed birthday party the week after Cal's diagnosis, friends and family had set up a fund at CHOP that had quickly raised ten thousand dollars. But since that money was controlled by the hospital, we would need our own 501(c)(3) nonprofit to raise money to support projects that reflected our family's wishes and would honor Cal. The foundation's board members were longtime friends, but they also brought rather extraordinary skills to the fledgling charity. There was Dr. Waldman, and Jill Cairns Milne, my former college roommate who had gone on to earn a doctorate at Harvard in biochemistry and is the CEO of a biotech firm in Boston working in the rare-disease space. There were two former students of Pat's and mine from our graduate student days at the University of Chicago: Rachel Kaiser is a physician who started her career in academic medicine at the University of California, San Francisco, and now was a successful rheumatologist in private practice based in Maryland; Riva Parker is a Yale Law School graduate and an attorney based in DC. Finally, there was Tim Bliamptis, a family friend. He and I hailed from the same hometown and had attended the same high school and church. My parents and his parents were close friends, and my dad helped Tim make some connections in Boston's closed world of finance back in the 1980s. Dad had even convinced his worried parents that Tim's plan to leave engineering to pursue a career in finance was not the disaster they feared it was. Tim has degrees from MIT and Wharton and was the founder of Weathergage Capital, an investment firm. For Tim, serving on the board was a way to repay the debt to my father.

Even though PJ clung to the idea that the doctors would be able to save his sister, we were not sure how we would use the money we raised. That winter we started selling cupcakes my focus was on children's hospice programs and a mural project at the hospital. Research was not something that interested Pat or me.

We christened our nonprofit the Calliope Joy Foundation—adding her middle name because the Calliope Foundation was already taken. It was a bit unwieldy from a branding perspective, but we needed to name the charity after Cal. A friend's daughter, Kaila Conti, who was a student at Drexel University studying marketing, hosted an event that raised two thousand dollars. After that, Al Lubrano, a reporter for the *Philadelphia Inquirer* who had interviewed me over the years for stories on poverty in Philadelphia, wrote a front-page story on Cal and our family. After that, checks from around the region came in, and we had soon raised another six thousand dollars. My friend Scott Charles nominated me for the Philadelphia Eagles' annual Community Quarterback award. We didn't win the grand prize of ten thousand dollars, but the four thousand dollars we received meant we had more than enough to get started.

We officially launched the foundation on Valentine's Day of 2013 with a bake sale at Saint Joseph's. Dave Allan, a colleague who teaches marketing at SJU, took pity on me and volunteered his students from the university's nationally ranked American Marketing Association to adopt our foundation for their annual service project.

The next event would be an inaugural Cupcake Challenge at PJ and Camille's elementary school in September 2013. Cal had been a frequent visitor at Cynwyd Elementary, and the principal and staff wanted desperately to help our family with the charity. They offered to let us use the school grounds for this event, though none of us knew what to expect.

Once the Saint Joe's students got involved, the tables were turned. After two decades of being a college professor, I was now being told what to do by a bunch of teenagers. The students hosted tutorials on the proper use of hashtags and the differences between Instagram, Twitter, and Facebook. My seventeen-year-old niece, Isabella, built the foundation's first website for her high school computer science class project.

During one of our planning meetings, half a dozen marketing majors and the president of a sorority who had taken one of my classes all insisted the foundation needed a step-and-repeat that would cost six hundred dollars. I'm someone who does not know the Kardashians' first names, and I certainly had no idea what a step-and-repeat was. The students relished explaining to me that it was a banner with logos for branding an event, typically used on the red carpet so all the photos of attendees could also promote sponsors. I remained unconvinced. They persisted, so we compromised, and one of their moms went to Staples and had a sort of tarp made with the foundation logo that we could tape on the wall. It was hideous, but on the day of the event dozens of people got their photos taken in front of it and posted selfies to social media with the hashtags #CalsCupcakes, #cures, and #cupcakes4Cal. "We told you so," Kaila explained when she showed me the foundation's new followers and social media traffic. Still, we would not purchase a proper step-and-repeat for another two years.

Starting a foundation means begging, lots of begging, and you need to keep in mind that every customer has a charity or a school or a cause. Businesses get dozens if not hundreds of requests. It was humbling going to bakeries and stores asking them to help us with an event for a child with a rare disease no one had heard of, but we had realized early on that being committed and crazy could be one and the same thing. The managers of Giant supermarket and the Wawa convenience store signed on, as did a local diner where Cal and I were regular customers. Maybe they felt sorry for us; maybe they just wanted us to stop bothering them for free stuff.

Now the first thing you need to know about working with cupcakes is that they are deceptively difficult to transport. They need to be packed carefully or they'll fall and get smashed and make quite a mess. And when you are dealing with two thousand cupcakes, moving them around is no small feat. Because they won't last, you need to find at least one thousand people who (1) want to eat a cupcake and (2) want to pay for it. On the health-conscious Main Line, where my friends avoid gluten and refined sugars with the same care they take with lead and asbestos, selling cupcakes for our cause would prove challenging.

After months of planning and hanging signs and decorating the gym at Cynwyd Elementary with the help of the local Girl Scout troop, the hour before we opened the gates was terrifying. The weather was perfect. Honestly, we had no idea if anyone would show up. What would we do with the two thousand cupcakes sitting in the school cafeteria if no one came? Pat was not worried; I suspected he secretly hoped Cal's Cupcake Challenge would bomb so he would not be dragged into any more of these wacky schemes.

With an hour to go Pat saw that a haze of panic was taking hold of me. He made me go home and arrange to bring Cal and her nurse over to the school. Besides, Pat was busy. He was fighting with the bounce-house rental company because the bounce houses kept deflating. When I left he was cursing at no one in particular as he searched for the cell phone number of the school custodian so he could have a generator delivered to the field.

By the time I returned with Cal more than an hour later, there were no empty parking spots near the school. One of the volunteers ushered me into a spot they had saved for us with orange cones. He explained, "The crowds started showing up when we opened the doors." All around, children and families filled the sidewalks bordering the school grounds. Friends and neighbors and the children's classmates and my coworkers from Saint Joseph's and Pat's colleagues from Rutgers University all made the trip out to support us that day. As a surprise, my sister Nicole drove down from Boston with her husband to be there. Two local television crews were setting up cameras at the main gate. By eleven o'clock in the morning a line had formed down the street. People we had not seen in decades had come out to be with us.

Pat and the volunteers had transformed the school into a magical carnival with balloons and face painters and cupcakes, thousands and thousands of cupcakes. Pat had brought a lawn chair from home, and he put it right at the main entrance where he sat with Cal in his arms. Cal greeted nearly everyone who came. Even Pat, who had resisted going public, was overwhelmed by how many of the parents of the boys and girls he coached left donations of twenty, fifty, one hundred, or five hundred dollars to support Cal's charity. My friend Julie had created a stunning display with information about leukodystrophy on a table right next to Pat and Cal. There were posters about the projects we had planned for the proceeds of the very first Cupcake Challenge.

The Challenge part of the event was Pat's idea. We would invite local children to bake and decorate cupcakes at home to be judged by professional bakers, in a kid-friendly version of the reality show *Cupcake Wars*. It was the heyday of the Magnolia Bakery and national cupcake-themed franchises such as

Crumbs, but we were unprepared for the popularity of the contest and just how seriously the kids (and their parents) would take it.

The first year of the Challenge, we had more than thirty entrants, including one young girl who came with her own fondant knife set. More than a few competitors took private lessons with professional pastry chefs. Another young baker incorporated a dry-ice element in her cupcake, and her mother brought in an accompanying video of the girl baking the cupcake so that there would be no questions from the judges. The same intensity that Main Line parents brought to sports and college admissions was being deployed in a cupcake bake-off for charity.

Dan Martino, the Cynwyd Elementary School principal looked forward to being a judge; he thought tasting a few cupcakes made by schoolchildren would be "fun." After the first dozen cupcakes, he and the rest of the judges understood they needed to stop swallowing if they were going to survive. When the prizes were given out and one little girl did not get a top award, her mother escorted the six-year-old to speak to the judges about why she had lost points and how she could place next year.

By the end of the day, Pat, our friends, and the volunteers were drained but in that wonderful sort of euphoric way. The school was a mess: there were frosting and crumbs and sprinkles everywhere. The school custodians who had the job of cleaning up after the event never uttered a word of complaint as they scrubbed blue frosting off every flat surface. The head of the community events team at CHOP, which had come to scout out the event, was impressed and encouraging, saying, "This is really good for your first effort." Pat looked at me, amazed at what Cal and our community had made possible and said, "I guess I know what you will have me doing every fall for the rest of my life." We were hooked.

The good news is that the events grew bigger and more successful and more ambitious over time. The Cupcake Challenge would spawn a Cupcake 5K, a Team Cupcake for marathon runners, and even a Cupcake Gala. Some failures that followed were far more memorable and taught us more about fundraising and why going out into the world to tell Cal's story mattered. Failure is the best teacher. As Robert Kennedy observed, "Only those who dare to fail greatly can ever achieve greatly."

After the Challenge's success, I proposed to Camille, my friend Lisa, and my neighbor Caryn that we plan to sell cupcakes outside a basketball game at SJU. The idea was straightforward enough (or so I thought)—we would sell a thousand donated cupcakes for one dollar each and raise one thousand dollars.

But the success of the Cupcake Challenge notwithstanding, finding that many people to do anything, even for a buck, is no easy feat. And in the era of credit cards, PayPal, and Apple Pay, most people don't carry dollar bills anymore. At the Challenge we had posters, and people knew our family's story. Even if they did not know about leukodystrophy, they understood that Cal had been impacted by a neurological disease. Total strangers at SJU did not know our story, and describing metachromatic leukodystrophy required an understanding of Greek and a medical dictionary. Standing in a parking lot selling cupcakes for a disease no one had ever heard of felt far from inspiring.

I doubt we sold one hundred cupcakes, and after a few hours it was clear that it was easier to panhandle for small change as a donation than to move the treats. The only reason university security did not remove me was because I flashed a badge and they recognized me as a faculty member. Students who passed by were perplexed—wondering why in the world Professor Kefalas, who enjoys a reputation on campus for being rather intimidating, was begging for money.

It's not clear why we kept going after the basketball game fiasco; maybe we were propelled forward by the eight hundred cupcakes sitting in the back of my minivan. (About the only upside was that the car smelled of butter and chocolate.)

The weather was cool enough for us to leave the cupcakes in boxes outside overnight, and Lisa suggested that we redouble our efforts at the Dickens Festival the next day. It was just before Christmas, and as a way to celebrate the holiday season without any overtly religious overtones, the nearby village of Narberth hosts a Dickens Festival. The mayor and the local shop owners take it all pretty seriously; they dress up in period costumes and, for a day, the town looks like an amateur theater company's set for *A Christmas Carol*. Besides, it was an excuse for local parents, who included more than a few faculty members at Penn and Villanova, to introduce their children to Charles Dickens. There was even a Dickens scavenger hunt with clues inspired by his books.

Lisa contacted the chamber of commerce and got permission to set up a tent at the festival. The organizers requested we dress up in period costume, so Pat found his wool coat and PJ got a magician's hat from a Halloween costume decorated with a plastic sprig of mistletoe that we tried to pass off as PJ playing Tiny Tim. We borrowed a tent and a table and made some signs and handouts. We were certain the Dickens Festival would be a far better venue for our fundraising. This crowd would be older, less intoxicated, and more family friendly.

The day of the festival, local meteorologists called for a light dusting of snow in the afternoon. When the first few flakes started coming down in the morning, Pat and I didn't worry. We had lived in Chicago for seven years and loved poking fun at our Philadelphia friends, who seemed to panic at the sight of a flurry. But very soon it was clear the snow would be no simple dusting—an inch was falling every hour, and it was accumulating, sticking on everything, ideal conditions for a ski resort in Colorado.

Quitting over a little snow still seemed silly. When I told Pat the festival looked more festive with the snow, he scowled in response. And as the snow intensified we found ourselves trapped because the roads were untreated and there were no plows out yet. The Dickens Festival most assuredly looked picturesque, and even Dickensesque as the actors performed period songs, but it would turn grim soon enough.

At least at the festival there were people old enough to still be carrying dollar bills. People asked about Cal and our charity, but as the snow got worse and people left we could not unload the cupcakes. By this time, the cupcakes (and the rest of us) were frozen solid. We stopped asking for money and began pleading with passersby just to take the cupcakes with them. People wanted to know if they were nut-free and gluten-free, and they were picky about the flavors. One woman only wanted one chocolate cupcake for her child. Another man picked through them to find a vanilla one.

What had been fun at 10 a.m. had become a nightmare by noon. We were hungry for real food, not cupcakes, and Pat Googled the symptoms of hypothermia on his phone. The only thing that brightened his spirits was going to a bar with a friend. A beer and a slice of pizza significantly improved his mood and saved our marriage that day. PJ seemed to have a great time, working the crowd, drinking hot chocolate, and polishing off a pizza, slice after slice. Years later PJ would say it was the most delicious pizza he ever ate, though pizza at a Dickens Festival is still anachronistic. At least it's possible Charles Dickens encountered a cupcake. It seems unlikely he ever ate pizza.

In those early days, a big hurdle for our fundraising was that we were not exactly sure what we should do with the money we were raising. The marketing students from SJU wanted us to tell a story, so we needed an elevator pitch. At first our plan was to create a mural at CHOP in honor of Cal, but it turned out that donating a piece of artwork to the hospital requires lots of approvals and coordination. What the CHOP Foundation could not diplomatically find a way to tell us was that the hospital rarely commissioned artwork. They really wanted us to give them a gift that would help with the construction of the Buerger Center, a new outpatient hospital facility. The CHOP

Foundation development team kept taking me out for coffee and lunches to pitch ideas for other projects, but the idea of putting Cal's name on a break room for nurses or a planter on the roof garden never felt right for the cupcake money.

In the end it was Cal's doctor, Amy Waldman, who would come up with the idea that would transform all of our lives.

It had taken me more than a year to pull out of the nosedive of my mental breakdown. For months after Cal's diagnosis my capacity to feel alive again might only flicker on and off like a short-circuited lightbulb. These momentary flashes where I could see colors or savor a kiss from my husband or remember what it felt like to find something funny proved that I was not beyond help or hope. It took months for that feeling to be sustained for a few hours. Sometimes, after a busy day at work, I might forget about what was happening to Cal. The hours grew into days and then even weeks when it seemed like I could rejoin the living. The early evidence of my resurrection was barely noticeable to anyone but me; at first I wanted to get my hair cut or buy new underwear or wear lipstick. These might not seem particularly noteworthy—when you are the walking dead, you see no point in using deodorant or flossing your teeth.

To this day Pat has a rule banning me from going out in public wearing pajamas and/or without proper undergarments. Full disclosure: this is a rule he probably must enforce at least monthly, even now. I needed to pretend to manage basic hygiene. Pat detested the UGG boots I taught in and wore to faculty meetings and the fact that all the pants I owned had elastic waists. More and more, bending down to tie my shoes was the only chance I had to see my feet, but no one talked about all the weight I had gained. Not even Pat brought it up, but Camille would occasionally purge the pantry of Oreos and peanut butter. My doctor encouraged me to try to keep my meals at around four hundred calories to see if we could get my weight "under control."

Despite this, the signs of life were there. I had even started writing, and one of the pieces I wrote about mothering a child with a terminal illness had gone viral for *Slate*. The cupcakes were curative; they helped me get out my own pain and grief and gave me a new purpose.

In July 2013, the anniversary of Cal's diagnosis had arrived, and I was transported back to the most terrible day of my life. Since I did not want Pat and the kids to see me weeping, I hid in our bedroom. All I could do was lie in bed watching videos of Cal from the time when our life was perfect. Visits to our old life, before Cal became the mermaid, were generally forbidden, but D-Day was a time for self-pity. There was Cal trick-or-treating dressed as a pumpkin, Cal sitting with my dad and eating French toast, Cal squealing with laughter and chasing after her brother. I pulled out the last pair of shoes Cal wore, her scuffed sandals. The sight of them made me cry so much it was like I was going to pass out.

I must have been searching the web for information about MLD when a link to an article in the journal *Science* popped up in the feed. I read the abstract, about a scientist and doctor named Alessandra Biffi, who, with her colleagues, had successfully treated three children with Cal's disease using a revolutionary gene therapy. After the treatment Dr. Biffi's patients showed no signs of MLD in their MRIs. The paper itself was so short it reminded me of the lab reports prepared by high school students: "The brain of this patient appeared normal two years after treatment. In contrast, the brain of an un-treated age-matched late infantile MLD patient showed severe demyelination and associated diffuse atrophy." The language was unremarkable, downright boring, yet the very understatement of it all seemed to goad me. There was no need for bragging—the children's MRIs were nothing short of miraculous.

My head was spinning. I called Dr. Waldman in a fury. A paper declaring that researchers had successfully treated three children with Cal's disease was not supposed to be published one year and sixteen days after she was diagnosed.

I actually wanted Dr. Waldman to tell me the whole thing was a hoax; the cowardly, selfish part of myself wanted to hear the work was a fraud. She would be my doubting Thomas, calling into question this alleged miracle. When we had first met a year ago, I had prepared myself for a gene therapy breakthrough in the next two decades, not now, while Cal was still living. The fact that the research was published in *Science* was a big deal. With a 4 percent acceptance rate and researchers from every discipline submitting papers, only groundbreaking and important findings appeared in the journal.

The truth is that no one was more astounded than Dr. Waldman. She had known about the research, but even the doctors in Milan had hoped only to leave the children with a milder form of the disease. No one expected clear MRIs. "This is a game-changer," Dr. Waldman declared, not even trying to hide her enthusiasm. "This gets me thinking: I know what you should do with the cupcake money: you need to help these families get to Milan for this clinical trial." This was not the response I had expected. Hope was an indulgence that Cal's disease had never granted us until it was too late to save her.

Despite our conversation from the previous year, at that moment I lacked the courage and generosity to consider helping other children when Cal could not be saved. "You have clearly mistaken me for a brave woman," I told Dr. Waldman. Then I started to sob again: "How could I have missed my chance to help Cal? We should have gotten on a plane to Italy, we should have tried harder to fight." In that moment, my superpower of grief evaporated. I doubted my capacity to be brave and generous and invest in other people's miracles.

But Dr. Waldman refused to accept this.

These families had paid a tremendous price for their miracle. Since gene therapy only worked to stop children from getting sick, it meant that after children were diagnosed it was too late to help them. The children treated in the Milan trial were the younger siblings of older kids who were already too sick for treatment. Once an older child got diagnosed, parents would be encouraged to do genetic testing of any younger siblings. If they found the disease in a younger child, then they were eligible for the trial Dr. Biffi was running.

The trial's success was tragically double-edged. It was an older child's illness that saved a younger sibling's life. "These parents will watch one child die. . . . Of course, you will help them," Dr. Waldman urged. Then she sighed. My guilt was misplaced. Dr. Biffi and her team in Italy had only treated *presymptomatic* children; Cal would have never been a candidate for the trial. MLD children can be diagnosed only after they show symptoms, when the disease has already done irreparable harm to the brain and central nervous system. No one can find MLD unless they are looking for the disease. Cal never had a chance. Gene therapy could not restore the damaged neurons; nothing could.

Of course, Dr. Waldman was right.

I knew it was a miracle that there were children who would go to preschool and eat birthday cake and hold their mothers' hands and walk across the street. I wanted to celebrate for these strangers, but I didn't know how to help in the shock of it all. Still, the fact that this news had arrived on the anniversary of Cal's diagnosis must mean something. Was this something amazing that Cal would be a part of? Could this be the miracle that Cal and the cupcakes were going to make possible?

In 1999, as a postdoctoral fellow at the University of Pennsylvania, I had a front-row seat to watch how the death of an eighteen-year-old clinical trial participant shuttered research at the school and nearly destroyed the reputation of James Wilson, once one of Penn's most respected and admired minds.

Jesse Gelsinger suffered from ornithine transcarbamylase (OTC) deficiency, a rare metabolic disorder that he managed with a low-protein diet and drugs, thirty-two pills each day. Like MLD, OTC deficiency is a monogenic disorder, the result of a single gene not doing its job.

Jesse was not sick, but he volunteered to test the safety of a potential treatment for the fatal form of the disorder in infants. "What is the worst that can happen to me?" he said to a friend before he entered the hospital. "I die, and it's for the babies." Gelsinger's therapy consisted of an infusion of corrective genes encased in a dose of a weakened cold virus, adenovirus, which functioned as what scientists call a vector. Vectors are like taxicabs that drive healthy DNA into cells. Viruses, whose sole purpose is to get inside cells and infect them, make useful vectors. The dosage he received had proven safe for mice, dogs, and another human, but it caused Jesse's immune system to go into overdrive, resulting in massive organ failure.

Jesse's death affirmed skeptics' worst fears about the hubris of researchers using viruses to repair genetic defects and overreaching scientists who put progress ahead of human life. Federal investigators determined that the researchers had not adequately briefed the eighteen-year-old on all the risks. His pre-op bloodwork indicated high levels of ammonia in his system, a finding that should have caused the team to halt the procedure.

Research protocols at all university hospitals were under increased scrutiny after Jesse's death and the lawsuit that followed. His family received a settlement rumored to be in excess of $10 million. More than that, his death would define the field for decades in the United States. Careers were ruined, and the federal government shuttered one of the nation's most distinguished medical institutions.

Industry money for gene therapy research dried up, most people believing that despite its early promise, it was too dangerous. Most of the research would come to be outsourced to other countries, where the public had never heard of Jesse Gelsinger. Very quickly, researchers in Europe were far ahead of their American counterparts.

In 2003, four gene therapy experiments led by a team in France were suspended because the treatment, which cured a three-year-old boy of a fatal immune deficiency (SCID, more widely known as the Bubble Boy disease), had a catastrophic side effect: cancer. The French researchers were about to declare gene therapy's first unequivocal success when two children in the study developed a form of leukemia. Scientists had long theorized that the retrovirus that was used as a vector could trigger cancer. The risk was that the virus, which integrates itself into the patient's DNA, could get lodged in or near cancer-causing cells. News that the first successful treatment had resulted in cancer in children was another setback to a field still reeling from Gelsinger's death.

Back in 1996, the Italian geneticist Luigi Naldini had proposed a different approach when he published a piece in *Science* in which he theorized that doctors could use the human immunodeficiency virus (HIV) to build a better vector. One of the challenges researchers had encountered in gene therapies was making the vectors deliver their cargo more quickly. It took months for the working copies of the genes to get to the cells, and the children with diseases like MLD did not have months to wait to slow down the disease.

The same properties that made HIV so lethal—the fact that it could infiltrate cells and tell them what to do—led Naldini to imagine that the virus could be tamed and used to build a more durable and fast-acting vector. You had to admire the daring behind repurposing a virus that had caused millions of deaths and so much suffering to save children. You could also see why the researchers were not taking their work public; the whole procedure sounded like the backstory to one of those zombie apocalypse movies. Even with vectors constructed from an inert form of HIV, doctors would still need to use high-dose chemotherapy to wipe out the children's immune system and then infuse patients with their own stem cells infected with a working copy of the broken gene that was killing them. Naldini wanted a way to transport the working copy of the gene so it would be integrated into the patient's body while making sure the transfer didn't activate a nearby cancer-causing gene.

When Naldini and his colleagues chose the diseases for which they would use their new HIV-derived vectors, they looked for disorders caused by a genetic defect that they understood and which could be repaired. A rare disease with no other treatments would provide the ethical calculus required for recruiting patients; no one would participate in a study if there were safer, approved therapies. Finally, the disease would have to be so terrible that parents would be willing to allow scientists the chance to test their work on their children. Some people wondered if parents would even be willing to submit to a treatment so fraught with risks and dangers.

Naldini asked Alessandra Biffi to run the MLD project. The team believed they had met two of three criteria to start treating babies. First, MLD had no other therapeutic options and most children died by the age of six. Second, a 2004 paper Biffi published had shown promising results. Dr. Biffi and her colleague successfully treated mice bred to have MLD. Using a modified stem cell transplant, the treatment targeted therapeutic genes to protect the central and peripheral nervous systems from MLD's most devastating effects.

By 2010, Dr. Biffi was ready to enroll patients for their first human trial, and one of the three children they would treat would be a one-year-old named Giovanni Price, from Omaha, Nebraska.

A my and Brad Price wed in 2004, and as they were devout Catholics who practiced natural family planning, Amy had given birth to five children in six years.

There had been no way to know that they were carriers of MLD until their third child, Liviana, was diagnosed at age two. The Prices' doctor at the University of Nebraska, William Rizzo, an expert in metabolic disorders, explained there was nothing to be done for Liviana. The good news was that Miles and Aria, Liviana's older brother and sister, did not have MLD, but nine-month-old Giovanni would need to be tested. They would have to wait a few weeks for the genetics expert to complete the screening and tell the Prices the baby had MLD too.

Finding a child with MLD is very rare—the odds are about one in forty thousand. It might happen only a handful of times in a doctor's career. Finding two siblings in the same family was devastating even for the most experienced physicians, such as Dr. Rizzo. It was like getting struck by lightning—twice. The double tragedy the Prices faced compelled him to think outside the box. There was no way to save Liviana, but the baby was different.

Most clinicians would not have known about the gene therapy trial that Luigi Naldini was about to launch in Italy, but Dr. Rizzo was on the board of the United Leukodystrophy Foundation, and he had followed the recent breakthroughs in the field. He had seen Dr. Biffi present her work with a mouse model and remembered that her team would be launching a human trial.

Dr. Rizzo was breaking ranks with the experts when he advised the Prices to go to Italy. Bone marrow transplants had been used for decades with children like Giovanni, but such a procedure was no cure, and there was a 30 percent chance it might kill him faster than the MLD. Many neurologists feared the Prices were making a tragic mistake going there.

The decision was fraught. Knowing one child would die but another could be saved created a blind, panicked urgency. They would never recover from the fact that Liviana could not be treated, but Amy and Brad came to believe that Liviana's purpose in life was to save her younger brother's life. Sacrifice was something God regularly required for miracles, after all.

The families enrolled in the trial at the San Raffaele Institute could get a small stipend to cover their expenses while they spent months away from home. Treating babies with gene therapy was still so new that the hospital didn't have cribs or hospital gowns for infants. Amy Price and Giovanni's nurses would dress him in a diaper and wrap him in blankets to be sure he didn't roll off the adult-sized bed.

The preparations for the treatment were just as complex as the treatment itself. Dr. Biffi and her colleagues manufactured the repaired duplicate gene using the patient's own homeopathic stem cells harvested from bone marrow. Then they built the most efficient and safest vectors they could by using the spare parts of HIV. Back in 2009 the manufacturing process was so cutting-edge that the scientists would walk the vectors from one side of the facility to the patients in the hospital wing. It was like building a plane while you are trying to fly it. Doctors were not even sure they could freeze the vectors safely to preserve them. The trick would be to make sure the child could accept the new gene without overloading the immune system or giving the child cancer.

Once the cells were made and the children underwent a barrage of MRIs, nerve conductivity testing, and blood work to determine a baseline for comparison so the doctors would know if the treatment was slowing the disease's progression, there would be four days of high-intensity chemotherapy to make room in the body for the repaired gene, which would be given to the children on the fifth day.

Gene therapy looks very much like a stem cell replacement, a procedure used for decades to treat blood cancers such as multiple myeloma and leukemia. The difference is that with stem cell treatments, patients receive their own stem cells, which are now cancer free, while in gene replacement therapy, patients get stem cells that have been infected with a working copy of the broken gene. After building the vectors, the most challenging part is making sure the body repairs the broken DNA.

Giving the children the vectors is the most straightforward step; it takes just a few minutes to infuse a small bag of fluids that looks like saline solution. The transfer of the corrected DNA causes the children no discomfort. On a day-to-day basis the biggest concerns are managing the risk of infection as a child's rebooting immune system makes the changes the vector wants and controlling the side effects from the chemotherapy. Children will become weak and tired and not want to eat, and they will develop painful sores in the mouth. While the cells come from the children's own blood and there is a far lower risk of rejection than from other kinds of transplants, the risk of infection is real, and it will take weeks before the children will be permitted to leave the windowless isolation rooms or breathe anything but the filtered air of the hospital.

Once Giovanni was admitted to the trial, Amy and Brad would travel back and forth to Italy, even bringing Liviana to the hospital in Milan. When they first arrived in Italy, one of the nurses asked why they had come there given that medical care is so much better in the United States. "That must not be true if we are here," Brad answered. In Italy, where Luigi Naldini is a household name, gene therapy is a cause célèbre with a glittering telethon on Italian television each Christmas. Unburdened by the controversy over Jesse Gelsinger's death, researchers such as Naldini and Patrick Aubourg in France had sprinted ahead of their American colleagues in gene therapy.[1]

The San Raffaele Institute may have been on the cutting edge of gene therapy, but it lacked the amenities found at Boston Children's Hospital or the Dana-Farber Cancer Institute. There was no Ronald McDonald House—the families were housed in a small hotel located over a Chinese restaurant. A dedicated group of volunteers tended to the families' needs and took them home for the holidays, but there were no child life specialists to prepare them for frightening procedures or kitchenettes on the hospital floors for making a cup of coffee. The families alternated between eating pizza from one restaurant and Chinese food from another. San Raffaele lacked video games, DVD players, and therapy dogs. The hotel's modest amenities were the free wireless service and a donated washing machine. The photos Amy posted on Facebook during those months purposely made the room she shared with children look like a hotel room on a holiday vacation. There were cheerful photos of Amy going to the park or market. But that was a mirage, her way of keeping her fears and the realities of the situation from Brad and their friends and relatives at home in Omaha.

Some days Giovanni was so weak from the chemotherapy that Amy worried he would not survive the doctors' efforts to save him. Having cared for Liviana and seen the MLD progress meant the Prices understood better than the doctors what this disease would take from Giovanni without the vector replacing his DNA. Yet Amy worried she had been selfish to gamble with her son's life this way: being in Italy meant squandering the "good time" on an unproven and unknown experiment no one dared call a cure.

Giovanni would need to return to Italy every six months. The good news was that the recovery time for the gene therapy was faster than for bone marrow transplants, so the children would resume their lives effortlessly, with baldness being the only sign of anything out of the ordinary. When the Prices returned to Milan after six months, Giovanni's first checkup showed that his arylsulfatase A enzyme levels were normal. But everyone knew Giovanni's real test would come in another six months, when he would be the age that Liviana had been when she got sick and they could see if the therapy had actually stopped the disease progression.

The Prices returned to Italy in 2012, and, miraculously, Giovanni's bloodwork and MRIs were mostly normal. One of the tests had picked up some neuropathy, but there was no sign of the MLD, and Giovanni seemed to have adapted to the nerve damage without any difficulty. He was doing so well that the physical and occupational therapists saw no reason to bring in support services. Giovanni and the other two children who had been treated also showed no signs of the dangerous side effects. The therapists told Amy that Giovanni would be able to enroll in school as a "healthy" and "neurotypical" child. He was deemed completely normal.

No one dared call Giovanni's treatment a cure, but it had given him much more than any other boy or girl with the disease had ever known: a healthy childhood.

Except for the other Milan families, most people had no understanding of the precise way the Prices lived. They savored every moment with Liviana as the disease marched on unstopped while letting Giovanni be a regular kid even though his normal childhood was the result of the most remarkable, if unproven, science. Giovanni's fate was filled with hope but plagued by uncertainty, while Liviana's situation was hopeless and certain.

During the summer of 2013, as Dr. Biffi published her findings in *Science*, Amy noticed that Liviana could no longer follow people or objects with her eyes. Amy and Brad guessed the disease was in its final stages. The hospice team advised them to start planning for Liviana's funeral, because they wouldn't want to have to worry about such details when their grief would be all-consuming.

Then something extraordinary happened. Amy learned she was pregnant for the sixth time, with fraternal triplets. She was forty-two. The doctors told her the chance of having triplets was one in three thousand. The pregnancy was unplanned. The Prices faced outrage from people who could not understand how they would go through with a pregnancy when they knew any child would have MLD.

That the Prices had become pregnant again as their daughter was dying made sense to me. As devout Catholics, they would never have ended the pregnancy. But more than that, watching Liviana die and seeing how Giovanni had thrived in the years after his treatment convinced them that the triplets were a gift, another miracle from Liviana. But many people could not understand how they would go through with a pregnancy given the risks. The dream of another child, with all the hope and possibility that represents, is so compelling in the face of death that rational thinking about the cruelties of the genetic lottery can easily be brushed aside. When your child is dying, you long to believe in angels, heaven, signs, fate, God's purpose, and meaning. Amy and Brad believed that this pregnancy with the triplets was a gift, that it was Liviana's way of helping them go on. The fact that there was a one in four chance that each baby would have MLD would not diminish that conviction.

Liviana died when Amy was eighteen weeks pregnant. The triplets, Cecilia, Christiano, and Roman, were born full term at thirty-eight weeks, weighing six pounds each. The triplets were tested as soon as they were born, but Amy and Brad had to wait another two months to learn if any of them had MLD. The good news was that the two boys, Roman and Christiano, were unaffected, but Cecilia had MLD. When Dr. Rizzo called to give them that news, this time the Prices knew exactly what to do. Dr. Biffi's team accepted Cecilia into the trial. She would be on her way to Italy as soon as the team in Milan was prepared to start treatments.

On Facebook I had stumbled onto the post that Amy Price had created to raise funds to get to Italy with Cecilia. The family was hosting a fireworks sale and auctioning items online to scrape together the money to go to Milan. There were people who questioned Brad and Amy's decision to give birth to another child who might have such a terrible disease, and I knew how hard it was to raise a thousand dollars. I sent an email to the fireworks fundraiser. The Calliope Joy Foundation's newly formed board immediately authorized a gift of two thousand dollars. Dr. Waldman was the first to respond, with a one-word text message that read "YES" in all capital letters.

The Prices were understandably cautious about this offer of help. Amy had not heard about us or our cupcakes. I sent her a text message: "Please tell me about Giovanni." I wanted to have another mother who knew what this disease could do tell me about what this gene therapy could do. I still doubted the mad scientists.

Amy messaged me back: "Giovanni is a normal boy."

"What does that mean?" I typed.

"Well, he is outside playing, I will try to make a video on my phone of him riding a scooter on the sidewalk."

"Is it a cure?" I asked.

"The doctors never call it a cure," she answered. This reminded me of what the doctors said about the stem cell replacement for Pat's cancer: it is a curative therapy; the disease was not gone, but it was stopped in its tracks, and the patient could reclaim a normal life. If the disease recurred, the doctors would just do another treatment. Pat's doctors had the same plan for his cancer as well.

Amy gave me permission to contact Dr. Rizzo. This was my due diligence—I needed to be careful about how we used this money. The Prices were getting ready to return to Italy and could use any help to get there. So what could it hurt to indulge me, some mother who might write a check? I emailed Dr. Rizzo, and his response appeared less than an hour later. It was just four sentences long:

> I sent Giovanni to Italy about three years ago and he is still asymptomatic. As you know, this is indeed a miracle. He was the second MLD child ever treated with gene therapy and he is still running around and playing like a normal boy. Now I look forward to Cecilia responding equally well when she gets treated.

I had studied this disease closely for two years. Giovanni should have been as sick as Cal by now, nonverbal, relying on a feeding tube, using diapers, paralyzed, unable to walk or speak. The *Science* paper only offered MRI scans. I longed to meet the children to see what gene therapy could actually do.

INVESTING IN MIRACLES

After that, things moved quickly. The seed we had planted with the Price family started to grow. I was always on the lookout for the next Cecilia. When newly diagnosed families contacted us, we would work quickly to see if there were younger children who might have the disease and benefit from gene therapy. With the magic of Facebook, either the families found us or I found them. Cal's cupcake money would soon help families from all over the world—the United States, Australia, England, Ireland, Australia, Slovenia, and Switzerland—to make the trip to Milan. By 2020 we had helped to send thirteen children to the gene therapy trials, granting them a chance at a miracle.

At home, in between teaching and caring for Cal, our nights and weekends were devoted to reaching out to parents, connecting them with doctors, helping them get genetic testing to confirm a diagnosis, and providing the support and guidance we had longed for when Cal was first diagnosed. My multiyear nervous breakdown had made me surprisingly adept at talking people off a ledge when they were grappling with the grief of diagnosis. There was something quite powerful about telling people that I knew they would be okay. My proof was that I could sit there and appear calm and rational. The mere fact that we were speaking was undeniable evidence of a parent's untapped courage: "If I can be brave, you can be," I promised.

Then I would share the best pieces of advice and lessons learned from Cal over the years.

Sometimes an intervention meant helping a family get passports or buying them a special adapter so they could charge their phones in Italy. There was the time I arranged for a family in Pakistan to send their child's blood and urine by courier to Philadelphia so that a lab at Thomas Jefferson University Medical School could confirm an MLD diagnosis. There was even a family from New Caledonia whom we helped make the nine-thousand-mile journey to see specialists in the United States.

When Amy Price wrote to tell me that the Italian hospital had no infant-sized hospital gowns, we found a volunteer with our hospice program to make them, and we shipped them to Milan. The gowns were decorated with dogs and cats and candy canes, and the nurses would send me pictures of the babies in the gowns. A retired Rutgers University administrator in New Jersey who had lost a granddaughter to leukodystrophy made pillowcases and quilts for all the babies, and whenever the doctors at CHOP diagnosed a baby, they would give a quilt to the family.

We would self-publish two illustrated children's books. The first explained leukodystrophy, and the second described gene therapy. While written for children, Dr. Waldman liked to read them to parents of newly diagnosed children when she needed the words to explain what the diagnosis meant. The idea for the books came from a schoolteacher in Pennsylvania. She had two brothers in her class with leukodystrophy and had written to ask if we had materials that educators could use to talk about the disease with children. The first book was dedicated to PJ and Camille, and it was basically an illustrated version of the words I had used to explain Cal's diagnosis to them. Perky Edgerton, the artist who had painted Camille's and Cal's portraits, had her daughter, Lela Meunier, illustrate the books for us. Every newly diagnosed family that reached out to me would get a copy, and some would buy several copies to donate to hospitals that treat leukodystrophy patients and their families. Over time we used the children's books when we spoke to journalists, policymakers, and potential donors, who tended to stare blankly when we talked to them about gene therapy and MLD. We translated the books into French, Spanish, and Polish and are planning Arabic and German editions.

The British pharmaceutical giant GlaxoSmithKline acquired the MLD gene therapy from the researchers in Milan in 2009, and the Cambridge, Massachusetts–based biotech company Bluebird Bio was running a successful clinical trial for the ALD gene therapy. They had licensed the French neurologist Patrick Aubourg's gene therapy for ALD. More companies were sniffing around clinical trials in so-called stealth mode. Shire (now Takeda) was working on an enzyme replacement therapy that doctors hoped would offer a bridge therapy to stabilize children and buy them time for gene therapy. Enzyme replacement therapy had proven quite effective in treating a host of lysosomal-storage diseases such as MLD. Millions of dollars of industry money were now chasing a cure for Cal's disease. Despite the small number of patients and the challenge of earning a profit treating such rare diseases, the promise of gene therapy was inspiring a gold rush mentality for industry and venture capitalists.

Not long after GSK invested in the MLD gene therapy research, the director of patient advocacy at GSK invited me to speak at the company's Pennsylvania headquarters in King of Prussia. Pharmaceutical companies regularly host such "patient-focused meetings" to allow researchers to interact with the patient community and learn the needs of the patients who will become consumers of their therapies. In the rare-disease community, working with the patient community is particularly crucial because finding patients poses unique challenges when just 3,600 babies are born with the disease each year. While it is unethical for the companies sponsoring clinical trials to interact with patients engaged in the therapy, like the Price family, it is permitted for patient advocates with a nonprofit or 501(c)(3) working on the front lines to offer advice and guidance. While speaking at GSK headquarters would be my first foray into the world of biotech and pharma, I began to speak frequently to pharmaceutical companies. I had the personal emails of biotech CEOs and world-renowned scientists.

Because of Cal we had been granted a front-row seat to the biggest medical breakthrough in a generation. When I received my invitation to speak with "the team at GSK," I imagined a meet-and-greet with a few dozen employees, perhaps the scientists in medical affairs and the patient-engagement and patient-advocacy folks. The day I arrived at the sprawling GSK campus I felt like Alice in Wonderland. The security officer handed me a badge with my photo on it, and I was escorted to a large auditorium. Behind the stage was a screen on the wall. A video crew was getting the stage set up with microphones, cameras, and lights. Years earlier I had done television spots with CNN and C-SPAN to promote the books I had published on my academic research. The video production crew at GSK was much more elaborate; it was the kind you would see at the studios for *Oprah* or *60 Minutes*.

I started to get a bit nervous and, trying to hide my growing anxiety, I wondered aloud, as casually as I could, "How large a crowd are you expecting?" "Oh, we expect fifty or seventy here in the auditorium," the patient-advocate liaison replied. That was fine, I thought. As a college professor, lecturing to a hundred people was part of my job description. Then she said, "But this talk is going to be simulcast in London and streamed to around forty thousand GSK employees around the world." I was taken aback, and I would have started to panic except that a professional photographer whisked me away to pose for a head shot and a member of the GSK public relations team interviewed me for their internal communications. The photographer asked me not to grin too much and said, "Your new brand is the brave mom." GSK even paid me a small honorarium of about four hundred dollars, which I donated to Cal's foundation.

During the fifteen-minute interview, I answered questions about Cal and all the things the disease had taken from her. I showed a video downloaded from my phone of Cal when she could walk and then a recent photo of her at home surrounded by our hospice nurses. Cal was seated on our couch where pillows and blankets were carefully arranged to keep her upright.

I talked about how Cal loves children's books and the BBC television show *Kipper*. And I stressed that, no matter what the medical literature said about MLD, it was not true that children like Cal suffered from dementia or were comatose. It was true that Cal could not speak, but she laughed and smiled and could recognize her father just by the sound of his footsteps.

I talked about the gene therapy families. I recounted the anguish of telling parents that the diagnosis of an older child had come too late but that this tragedy would make it possible for them to save a younger brother or sister. There were stories about two mothers' courageous decisions to continue with pregnancies even after they learned the children they carried had MLD. We discussed the new lexicon the families had invented to describe what gene therapy is. As a parent advocate, I said, "I never use the word 'cure.'" Indeed, "We do not know what gene therapy means for patients, how long it will last, and what it can do for diseases like MLD. But the way it changes children's lives is a miracle. In the best cases children are saved from MLD's most catastrophic effects. When gene therapy works, it is like slamming the brakes on this nightmarish disease."

Thinking about the families and about Cal, I lost my composure. I explained how grateful I was for this clinical trial and how it had changed my life. I had come to see myself as the luckiest unlucky woman in the world. "We cannot save my daughter Cal," I said, "but we will get to see a different ending to other children's stories." Each time a family sends a photo of a child singing or walking or going to kindergarten, our family gets to share in that family's miracle.

There was something about being at GSK that made me think the people who worked there needed to understand how transformative their work was. They needed to see what it meant to our families.

Then I realized that my mascara (on this rare occasion when I wore makeup) was running down my face, and my eyes were swollen and red. The fact that I now bore a striking resemblance to Tammy Faye Bakker didn't seem to matter to the thousands of people around the world watching me tell our story. The superpower of grief was touching the people in that room and even in London and Tel Aviv. It was transforming them on a cellular level. I believed they could understand how much we had lost, and they could see and feel what this research meant to the families. I told them, "I wish you all could witness the miracles you have made possible. I wish you could see these beautiful children leading a life that was supposed to be impossible."

When it ended, I felt as though I was waking up from a trance. I think the audience gave me my first standing ovation. The event moderator in London, the head of GSK's rare-disease program, seemed to compose himself. "Maria, I must tell you, there is not a dry eye here in London. Now, whenever I watch *Kipper* with my own daughters, I will think of your Calliope."

It turns out GSK employs a vast number of people, many of them in its Philadelphia headquarters, and for months afterward, employees would stop me in the market or the street. A mother I met at school who worked in GSK's legal affairs department approached me to say, "I saw your talk. Thank you for reminding me why my work matters. This is bigger than a new asthma medication. This is different." Another man ran up to me in the Trader Joe's parking lot and explained he was part of the regulatory-affairs team. He was overcome with emotion. "I am a father . . . and the MLD gene therapy research is the best thing I have been a part of in my twenty years in the industry. I doubt I will ever do anything else so important."

At the Children's Hospital of Philadelphia, Cal and the cupcakes had changed Dr. Waldman's life too. We now spoke regularly on the phone or communicated via email and text. Pat joked that I now was an unpaid employee of CHOP. Dr. Brenda Banwell, the chief of neurology and an expert in myelin disorders in children, agreed that the time was right to launch a Leukodystrophy Center of Excellence at CHOP. The breakthroughs in gene therapy—and new laws in Pennsylvania, New York, and New Jersey mandating screening for globoid cell leukodystrophy (or Krabbe disease) and adrenoleukodystrophy (ALD) at birth—meant children could be monitored and treated over their lifetimes. The time was right for this bold new initiative, and Dr. Waldman had been tapped to be the center's first medical director.

It was astounding to see the idea to launch a center catch fire. We had not raised millions of dollars or donated a new building to the hospital. We just had the cupcakes, Cal, and a woman possessed by the notion that her daughter's life mattered. It was the superpower of grief at work once again. More and more, Cal was living up to her namesake, Calliope, Homer's muse of poetry and song. Cal seemed to possess the magical power to cast spells. How else could you explain how the senior leadership of one of the finest children's hospitals in the world decided to change course and invest millions of dollars in resources and people to defeat leukodystrophy? This was a big deal.

Dr. Waldman could not contain her excitement: "I can't get into too many details but the enthusiasm around this is nothing like I have ever witnessed here at CHOP," she said. When Dr.

Waldman sent out emails to announce a meeting, she might expect four people to attend; then she would need to relocate to a larger room to accommodate the eight who showed up. "More and more people come to the meetings each time," she told Pat and me. Colleagues in complex care, pediatrics, palliative care, metabolics, rehabilitation medicine, hematology/oncology, and the blood and bone transplant program—as well as neurology and gene therapy research—wanted to be a part of this center dedicated to children with leukodystrophies.

And it was not just doctors from CHOP. A postdoctoral fellow at the University of Pennsylvania's School of Veterinary Medicine had been doing research on lysosomal-storage disorders with the remaining funding from an NIH grant. She had created a canine model for globoid cell leukodystrophy. That this crucial work was taking place a few blocks from CHOP was like winning the lottery; normally it would take years and millions of dollars to create an animal model for clinical trials.

At the University of Pennsylvania's Orphan Disease Center (ODC), none other than Jim Wilson had learned about Dr. Waldman's meetings. Despite Dr. Wilson's complicated past and the questions that had lingered in the wake of Jesse Gelsinger's death, he remained a legendary figure at the University of Pennsylvania, known as a brilliant scientist and a visionary. Whether you admired Wilson or were one of his detractors, everyone agreed that his research was revolutionizing medicine. The ODC, where Wilson had spent his years as a "refugee," was a well-resourced and influential program despite the fact that it largely worked below the radar. Hundreds of people worked in the Wilson lab; the most brilliant doctoral and medical students sought fellowships with him. I have never met Dr. Wilson, but I have heard him speak over the years. He is a commanding presence.

Wilson could see that the breakthroughs in treating leukodystrophy and other neurodegenerative disorders offered an opportunity to redeem gene therapy's reputation. Treating neurodegenerative disorders like MLD would be game-changing, so it made sense that Wilson had a vested interest in seeing CHOP become home to such a program. It was a badge of honor at the University of Pennsylvania, where CHOP and Penn are partners and rivals simultaneously, that Dr. Wilson would lend his support to the program by providing a Kickstarter grant. Wilson's involvement would be the spark, igniting the support to make the center an institutional priority.

While Dr. Wilson's involvement was crucial, Dr. Waldman and her boss, Dr. Banwell, preferred to give the credit to Cal and to families like ours. "None of this would have happened without you and Cal. None of it." Each time Dr. Waldman said this, I would run home and tell Cal how my sweet girl was changing the world and helping so many other children.

There was no question the timing was perfect.

More than a decade after Jesse Gelsinger's death, researchers at the same hospital in the same city would put gene therapy back on the map again with another child who had gotten a happy ending to her story. Just two months before Cal's diagnosis at CHOP in 2012, a seven-year-old cancer patient named Emily Whitehead became the first child to be enrolled in a clinical trial for patients with B-cell cancers such as acute lymphoblastic leukemia (ALL). At the University of Pennsylvania, researchers such as Dr. Carl June pioneered the idea that doctors could harness cell therapy to construct a synthetic immune system designed to recognize and kill cancer cells. Cell replacement and gene replacement therapies both use viral vectors constructed from HIV.

Dr. June and his colleagues treated Emily Whitehead by using the naturally occurring parts of the immune system called B cells and T cells as building blocks. T cells have evolved to kill cells infected with viruses, and B cells are the cells that make antibodies that are secreted and then bind to kill bacteria. Dr. June used the vectors constructed from HIV, he said, "as a Trojan horse to get past the T cells' immune system."[1] CAR T-cell therapy was "a chimera, a fantastic fire-breathing creature from Greek mythology with a lion's head, a goat's body, and a serpent's tail. The virus also inserts genetic information to activate the T cells, programming them into their killing mode."[2]

The treatment worked, but, tragically, the side effects were killing Emily.

By day three, Emily was comatose and on life support after kidney and lung failure. It was like Jesse Gelsinger all over again, and fear was rampant that the University of Pennsylvania would be the site of yet another tragedy. Emily's fever was as high as 106 degrees Fahrenheit for three days, and the team did not know why.[3] Standard blood tests revealed no infectious cause for her fever, but the bloodwork showed Emily had elevated levels of a protein called interleukin 6, or IL-6. In fact, the protein was more than a thousand times above the normal levels.[4] A few months before Emily was admitted to the hospital, Dr. June, whose daughter had pediatric arthritis, had read about a new drug approved by the FDA to treat elevated levels of IL-6 called tocilizumab.[5]

Out of desperation and left with no other options, the hospital's institutional review board and Emily's family agreed to use the tocilizumab, a drug that was not part of the original clinical trial protocol. The results were nothing short of striking: within hours, Emily began to improve rapidly. Twenty-three days after her treatment, she was declared cancer-free, and today she's fourteen years old and still in remission. Whitehead's story would redeem Wilson and his colleagues, a small group of true believers who had pursued cell and gene therapies after so many had declared the field dead. Philadelphia was ground zero for this work, so much so that industry boosters rebranded the Philadelphia biotech sector "Cellicon Valley."[6]

It would take just six months for the Leukodystrophy Center of Excellence at CHOP to be launched.

At the breakfast to announce the new center, the speakers featured a host of dignitaries, including CHOP's physician in chief, the division chief of neurology, the head of the bone transplant and blood marrow transplant program, the head of the newborn screening program, and several members of the neurology and metabolics faculty. I could not even imagine the complex scheduling that was required to get all these important people in the same room in the middle of the week. Amy Waldman was the first person to speak, and she introduced the program's other speakers. Among the invited guests was Jim Wilson. By the time CHOP launched the Leukodystrophy Center, Dr. Wilson's research with a biotech company called AveXis had shown tremendous promise in treating another devastating neurological disorder in children known as spinal muscular atrophy, or SMA. (That research would lead to FDA approval of Novartis's Zolgensma, one of the most expensive but impressive drug therapies in history.)

That morning Dr. Wilson gave a brief overview of the University of Pennsylvania's gene therapy program, highlighting the Orphan Disease Center's progress in treating a form of inherited retinal blindness. (Two years later, this work made history when the FDA granted approval for Spark Therapeutics' Luxturna, the first gene therapy to treat an inherited disorder.) During his talk Dr. Wilson showed a photo of the dog that they had treated for blindness. He recounted how they had taken the dog to meet with policymakers on Capitol Hill to convince them that gene therapy was safe and effective. He joked how the politicians enjoyed meeting with the dog more than with him and the other scientists.

Then, all of sudden, Wilson paused. He went off script for a moment: "There are seven thousand rare diseases," he said. "We will not cure them all, but Dr. Biffi's work in MLD is stunning, and MLD will be defeated." Amy Waldman, beaming, turned to find me in the crowd. At that moment, if I had not been seated I might have fallen down. I started to weep tears of joy and relief and amazement. Pat grabbed my hand tightly; he was proud of our family, the cupcakes, of Cal, and even proud of me, his crazy, maddening, and determined wife who had forced him to sell cupcakes in a blizzard.

Wilson finished his talk to a loud round of applause, and a crowd engulfed Pat and me. By the time I could break free, Dr. Wilson had disappeared. I never got the chance to thank him. This is probably a good thing, as he did not strike me as the type of person who appreciates emotional outbursts from an overwrought woman. But I ran back to Dr. Waldman and hugged her and said, "Thank you for believing in Cal. Thank you for making this possible."

When the new Leukodystrophy Center opened, Dr. Waldman and her team insisted that Cal be its very first patient.

While Dr. Waldman was moving mountains at CHOP, I came up with another insane idea.

Cal and I were watching a piece on CBS News about the NFL legend Jim Kelly, the former quarterback of the Buffalo Bills, and I suddenly thought that we should invite him to headline a gala for the leukodystrophy center. Kelly is beloved by football fans for calling his own plays and never whining about losing the Super Bowl four years in a row. And while other players might have left Buffalo for greener (and warmer) pastures, Kelly remained loyal to his adopted home.

His football triumphs notwithstanding, tragedy seemed to follow Kelly. This, most assuredly, resonated with me. Football fans felt for him after his son, Hunter, died at the age of eight from a form of leukodystrophy called Krabbe disease. Kelly's own battle with oral cancer had captured international attention when his oldest daughter, Erin, a college freshman, posted a touching photograph of herself lying beside her father in a hospital bed as the pair watched a football game. The Instagram post immediately went viral, with millions of fans using the hashtag #Kellytough.

"Kelly tough" had been the quarterback's mantra as a player and through the travails of his life. But it was in his Hall of Fame speech that he paid beautiful tribute to his only son, who would die not long after his induction:

> My only son, Hunter, was born on February 14, Valentine's Day, my birthday. The son I've always wanted. I've dreamt what every father dreams about: playing catch in the backyard, going fishing, camping, everything that fathers and sons do. But within four months my son was diagnosed with a fatal disease called Krabbe leukodystrophy. They told us to take him home and make him comfortable. And from that day, my wife and I decided to fight this disease. And so, we made it our lifelong commitment to make sure that kids all over the world don't suffer like my son does. Since the day I was selected [for the Hall of Fame], I prayed to God that my son would be here with me today. God has granted me that blessing. It has been written throughout my career that toughness is my trademark. Well, the toughest person I've ever met in my life is my hero, my soldier, my son, Hunter. I love you, buddy.

Since Cal's diagnosis I had come up with all kinds of nutty ideas. I tried to invite the comedian Adam Sandler to sing a song he had performed on *Sesame Street* for Cal. When we enrolled in a children's hospice program (one of the nation's four programs to care for terminally ill children, housed at Abington-Jefferson Hospital), I wrote a letter to Catherine, Duchess of Cambridge, who is the honorary spokesperson for children's hospice in England, asking her to come to Pennsylvania and meet Cal when she toured the United States. And then of course there were my numerous letters to Vice President Joe Biden asking him to meet Cal and tell me how he had survived the loss of his wife and daughter and then the death of his son from a glioblastoma.

But asking Jim Kelly to attend the gala actually seemed achievable, at least to me. There were so many parallels between our family and the Kellys. Both Jim and Pat had cancer, and we both had children who suffered from leukodystrophy; it all made perfect sense in the same way a stalker is convinced that the object of their obsession is destined to fall in love once they have the chance to meet. We would host a glittering gala to support the newly launched center, and Kelly would be the big name to draw a crowd. So I called my good friend Ashley Fox, a journalist with ESPN. PJ and Ashley's daughter Ella had attended the same preschool, and Ashley was one of those friends who had stayed close and offered her support when Cal got diagnosed. I knew she was on a first-name basis with nearly everyone in the NFL and might actually have a personal connection to Kelly. Much to my surprise, Ashley did not know Jim Kelly, but she knew his publicist. Within a day, she passed on a phone number.

Ashley thought this plan to get Jim Kelly likely would go nowhere. He was a Hall of Fame quarterback who charged upward of twenty-five thousand dollars for a one-hour appearance, and his schedule was booked months or years in advance. Since the "Kelly tough" story broke, Jim had been featured in the national media on CBS and ESPN. Ashley knew about all the people who want a piece of a man like Jim Kelly. But she wanted to help if she could. An optimist, she cheered me on, saying, "Maria, if anyone can pull this off, it might be you." I never doubted it for a moment. The Kelly family understood the superpower of grief better than anyone.

Not long before falling ill, Jim Kelly had met with the governor of Pennsylvania to lobby state officials to include Krabbe disease in the state's newborn screening program. Newborn screening is the heel-prick blood test that all children are given at birth.[7] Most parents who take home healthy children hardly even notice the nurses collecting blood on little pieces of cardboard. But newborn screening is one of the biggest public health initiatives for children after vaccinations. Experts believe twelve thousand children's lives are saved each year through the screening, which identifies dozens of inherited and metabolic disorders that are invisible at birth but are treatable if caught in time. In the leukodystrophy community, newborn screening is a major priority because promising treatments such as gene therapy work only if children can be identified before they get sick; nothing can repair the damage to the brain and central nervous system.

In the years after Hunter's death, the Kelly family had created the Hunter's Hope Foundation to push states to screen for Krabbe disease at birth. The foundation's annual family conference in upstate New York is a beloved event in the leukodystrophy community. A new law for newborn screening—Hannah's Law[8]—that Jim Kelly had championed was expected to go into effect in Pennsylvania in a few months. Kelly would want to come to Philadelphia to take a bow for newborn screening, I thought. We just needed to convince him to attend.

It turned out that the timing proved perfect. Not only was Jim on the mend from his cancer treatment, but more important, the Kellys were about to launch a book tour for Jill and Erin Kelly's new memoir, *Kelly Tough*. So I convinced the Kelly family's gatekeepers (who included Jill Kelly's mother, Jacque, who is the executive director of Hunter's Hope and also managed the family's publicity for the book tour) that this gala would be a win-win, helping the hospital and getting the family to Philadelphia just as they were on the book tour.

Jacque drove a hard bargain. Our foundation would cover all the costs and be responsible for selling the tickets and getting the sponsorships, and Hunter's Hope would be listed as a cosponsor and would take a share of the auction proceeds. Jacque offered a truly brilliant idea for the fundraiser: we would auction off the chance to catch a football thrown by Jim Kelly. Pat and Ashley were confident the football fans in the room would pay good money to live out their Super Bowl fantasy of catching a pass from a Hall of Fame legend.

Sometimes the superpower of grief steered me into perilous waters. Let me just say that hosting a charity gala is a high-risk venture; the vast majority of such events fail miserably. The head of CHOP's events team requested a phone meeting. At first I had assumed they wanted to lend their support and congratulate us, but the truth was they were staging an intervention. Selling cupcakes in a school playground was one thing, but galas were another matter altogether. The head of the community events team explained that CHOP already hosted half a dozen major events in the city every year. And with only fifty-two weekends in a year, on any given weekend in any US city, there are at least one or two events taking place. They didn't want the competition, and they were worried we would fail.

The people at the CHOP Foundation warned, "You will be lucky to break even." They were right, most galas do not survive beyond their first year, but we had Jim Kelly, this was destiny, and we could make it work. At the time we had about $25,000 in the foundation's checking account, just enough for a down payment on a hotel ballroom but not enough for a charity event.

That February I booked the ballroom at one of Philadelphia's poshest hotels, the Rittenhouse. I ordered the tickets and picked out a menu. The problem that I had not quite appreciated was selling those tickets. As college professors, Pat and I did not swim in the same circles as the city's donor class. We had a few friends who would purchase tickets and maybe a table for two thousand dollars, but without the five-thousand- and ten-thousand-dollar sponsorships, we would need much more money just to break even and fill the seats.

That's when I reached out to an MLD father I had met just once. Matt Hammond and his wife, Lauren, had a daughter, Loie, with MLD. Loie and Cal had been diagnosed months apart, and the Hammonds lived about twenty-five miles from us, in Chester County, Pennsylvania. Loie had succumbed to MLD just a year after her diagnosis. I had read about the Hammonds on Facebook when someone in the MLD community posted a beautiful story about the family. They had spent a year believing Loie had cerebral palsy, but when her symptoms became worse, the family learned that Loie was not disabled but terminally ill. By the time they realized Loie had MLD she was too ill to take a Make-A-Wish vacation. With the money from Make-A-Wish, Lauren and Matt decided to build a garden for Loie—with a gazebo and wind chimes and a little fountain. Loie had gone blind, and Matt and Lauren would spend twelve to sixteen hours a day just holding her. The garden was a beautiful and peaceful place where they could sit out in the sun. The story had appeared in the local paper, and I had fallen in love with Loie and the Hammonds right away.

After Loie passed away, I reached out to the Hammonds and invited them to the Cupcake Challenge. I was not sure they would come, as they were still mourning Loie, and it was hard for them to go out in public and meet other families. Much to my surprise, they came. Matt's mom, Christine, had pushed them to go out and meet another family like ours. Matt and Lauren said almost nothing at the Challenge, but they took it all in. Loie's brother Owen seemed smitten with Cal because she was so similar to his sister.

In February 2014, as I worked on the fundraiser, I reached out again. I wrote to see if Matt would be interested in helping with the gala. I figured he might have a few friends and neighbors who would want to come out and support the cause. I hoped he would sell a few tables and help us break even. What happened next saved the gala and the foundation and brought me one of my dearest friends.

Matt is far more practical about money than I am, and he certainly knew the idea was probably crazy, but he wanted in. It turned out that I had found another parent who understood the superpower of grief. Matt came to believe that the timing of my request, right on the anniversary of Loie's passing, was a sign. This was something he could do to make a difference, to harness his pain to accomplish something wonderful to help children in his daughter's name.

The day we met at the Cupcake Challenge, he had been uncharacteristically quiet, as he was thinking about Loie. I doubted we would ever meet again. Families grieve differently; for every parent who wants to start a foundation and raise money and host galas, many more have little interest in sharing their stories or raising money. Most parents who bury their children keep their grief close. There is no single way to grieve, and I had assumed that Matt and Lauren might not want to share Loie with others. But that day was an exception.

Pat and Lauren like to joke that Matt and I formed the most inexplicable friendship and partnership. Matt is tall, fit, handsome, and an absolute extrovert. In high school he was the popular kid and was voted prom king. I was the teacher's pet who could not find a date for the prom. Matt runs a very successful engineering business in West Chester and works with developers and corporate clients ranging from car dealerships to billion-dollar companies like GSK. Fifteen years my junior, he is a probusiness/small-government Republican active in Chester County politics who is on a first-name basis with US senator Pat Toomey. We have nothing in common except a limitless love for our daughters who shared a terrible diagnosis.

The bond we shared may have been unlikely (if not impossible), but a parent's grief transcends place, time, temperament, politics, and personality. Matt agreed immediately to help with the gala. And unlike most other people, he had no doubt we could pull it off. He was all in with my wacky plan. He wanted to be a part of it despite the pretty high likelihood we would fail. After each phone call we would say the same thing to each other: "We are doing this for our girls."

Not long after we finished our first meeting and Matt signed on, he composed a letter. It had been just a year since Loie's passing, and friends and colleagues and family regularly offered to help. Matt had declined these kindnesses when Loie was ill and after her death. A proud and private man, he did not want to take advantage of his friends and colleagues. There was nothing they could do to change what Loie's loss meant to the family.

But now Matt saw how he could transform the condolences and offers of help into meaningful action. His letter was an extraordinary document, addressed to friends, colleagues, neighbors, and family. It talked about his anguish over the loss of Loie and the chance he had been granted to help other children and families in her name. He described the gala as something his love for his daughter called him to do. So now he was reaching out to all the people who had offered their help. If what they had said at the funeral were not just empty words, he would welcome their support now. While Matt never would have asked people to help him take care of his family, it was easy to ask them, in Loie's name, to help kids like her.

The response was stunning. From the start Matt was confident he would sell the tickets, but I don't think any of us anticipated what he could accomplish. Each Friday the white envelopes with checks enclosed would arrive from Matt. One of the first checks we received was from the Chester County Republican Party. Back then we were in the dark ages of event planning, so Matt and I did everything by email and Excel spreadsheets. For that first gala we did not even have a way to process credit cards. It was a mom-and-pop operation, just two strangers consumed by a deranged idea that people had tried to talk us out of doing.

The first envelope had two thousand dollars, then it was four thousand dollars, and there were weeks when it was ten thousand dollars or twelve thousand dollars, and the money just kept coming. The moment the envelopes arrived I would bring them over to the bank. We had raised close to one hundred thousand dollars and sold more than three hundred tickets. When I would call to check in with Matt and thank him for his great work, he would always say, "I am doing this for Loie."

Two months before the gala we had to tell people we could not get them a seat: we were sold out.

On the night of the gala we all stood in awe of what we had managed to pull off in five months. There were tables of donated items from the Philadelphia 76ers, Eagles, and Phillies; a purse from Kate Spade; a gold necklace from a New York designer; and a pearl choker from a Main Line jeweler. US senator Bob Casey had agreed to serve as the honorary chair. Kansas City Chiefs coach Andy Reid, another friend of Ashley Fox who had just lost a son to a drug overdose and seemed to understand the superpower of grief, sent a signed helmet from the Chiefs for the charity auction. Kristin Roosevelt, an executive at Thermo Fisher Scientific and a close friend of Matt and Lauren Hammond, did a full-court press on her colleagues to get them to become a presenting sponsor at an event no one had heard of. Matt had charmed the biggest land developers in the state into writing checks. Because Matt had constructed dozens of Wawa convenience stores in the state, the Wawa Foundation became a sponsor.

Because of Dr. Waldman our guests included Howie Roseman, the executive vice president and general manager of the Philadelphia Eagles. With Jim Kelly headlining the event, Ashley invited Bill Polian, the Hall of Fame general manager who led the Buffalo Bills to four consecutive Super Bowls, to speak and asked ESPN reporter Sal Paolantonio to be the master of ceremonies. Former Eagles great Ron Jaworski and the governor of Pennsylvania had sent their regrets about missing the night. Matt and I had planned the whole evening with a handful of friends, the catering staff at the hotel, and a portable file folder purchased at Staples, filled with Matt's spreadsheets. We had not even hired an event planner. The flowers had been donated by Giant supermarkets. Even Liz Scott wanted to volunteer; she helped run the registration table to check in the guests.

When Jim and Jill Kelly took to the stage and told the story of their son Hunter, they received a standing ovation. Jim thrilled the crowd by tossing footballs through the Rittenhouse's elegant ballroom. The catering staff looked ashen as the footballs arced dangerously close to the massive crystal chandelier, which swayed back and forth as Jim's perfectly aimed throws whizzed by.

The event would make an eighty-thousand-dollar gift to CHOP's new center possible. There was a touching write-up in the *Philadelphia Inquirer*. The local sports-radio programs featured the event in their coverage. The CHOP Foundation development staff could not believe we had pulled it off. Howie Roseman wrote a personal note to Matt telling him what an inspiration he was. As the father of four children he hoped he would have Matt's courage in the face of such tragedy.

It was such a success that everyone wanted to know when we would do another gala. Roseman and the Eagles were so impressed that they insisted we host the next gala at Lincoln Financial Field, where the team plays. I told Matt of my idea to have the children who had undergone gene therapy get up on stage and toss out footballs as "quarterbacks for a cure."

"Matt, think of it, a stage full of kids with leukodystrophy who should be in wheelchairs and using feeding tubes running and throwing footballs." Matt nodded. I was reminded of a joke the comedian Chris Rock had told. As a kid, like so many of us, Rock had watched the Jerry Lewis Labor Day Telethon for muscular dystrophy. And in all those years, Rock noted, not one kid had walked on stage with Lewis. Because of gene therapy, we had dozens of children who were not supposed to walk on stage but could.

The following years brought all manner of miracles, great and small. Cal's foundation would grow, and so would the center she helped build at CHOP.

Back when Cal was diagnosed, CHOP had just one hundred leukodystrophy patients and there was no research on the disease taking place at all. That changed forever in 2016 with the arrival of Dr. Adeline Vanderver, who would be lured from Washington, DC's Children's National Hospital with an endowed chair. Vanderver is originally from Belgium, speaks three languages, has degrees in neurology, biochemistry, and genetics, and quite simply knows more about leukodystrophies than nearly anyone else on the planet. Vanderver's move to Philadelphia instantly made CHOP a global leader in leukodystrophy research. This was huge, not simply because of the work she had done but because of what it meant for the training of the next generation of scientists and doctors who would treat kids like Cal. Her arrival in Philadelphia was like an accelerant, and being at CHOP meant Vanderver had the resources to build incredible global partnerships. In Philadelphia she would have access to billions of biotech dollars that could transform her research into viable therapies.

In 2013, while at Children's National, Dr. Vanderver founded the Global Leukodystrophy Initiative (GLIA). Back then its conference was a modest event with twenty attendees. The 2019 GLIA conference, hosted by CHOP, gathered hundreds of researchers, scientists, and industry leaders from around the globe. Jim Wilson was one of the attendees and sponsors of the event.

CHOP was now hosting conferences for patient families. Families who had never met another child with their condition were making the trip there to find answers and hope, both of which had seemed impossible just a few years earlier. It enraged Dr. Vanderver and Dr. Waldman when newly diagnosed families were told to go home and enjoy the time they had left. "What other sort of diseases get that sort of response?" Dr. Vanderver would say. There was no longer any reason to suggest to families that "there is no treatment" or that "there is nothing to be done." CHOP really had become the place "where hope lives."

Over the next few years, families from around the world who needed help contacted the foundation. We got a call from Dr. Vanderver to help relocate a family from California to Philadelphia so their baby could be enrolled in a clinical trial. Without the treatment Dr. Vanderver's team could provide at CHOP the baby might die in a matter of days or weeks. Another couple had driven up to Philadelphia from West Virginia with a sick baby on a feeding tube and was sleeping in their car, and we got a call asking for funds to get those parents money for a hotel room.

When kids like Cal arrive at CHOP's state-of-the-art Buerger Center, a team of thirty-five specialists collaborates on caring for them. CHOP's Leukodystrophy Center of Excellence would grow to see forty leukodystrophy patients a month and house ten clinical trials and research studies that would attract patients from around the world. In 2017, Dr. Laura Adang, an MD and PhD from the University of Virginia, came to work with Dr. Vanderver. Within two years Dr. Adang was overseeing the largest ALD newborn screening clinic in the country, treating children identified at birth with the Lorenzo's Oil disease and working to ensure that those who once died by adolescence now got a chance to lead long, healthy lives. In 2019, the clinic received an NIH grant for five million dollars.

It is not clear how any of it would have happened without our Cal, our beautiful girl, our magical mermaid who has inspired so much good in the world and helped so many other children even though she would not be saved. Cal has taught me that when the worst possible thing happens, you have nothing left to fear. She has taught me that fearless people are maddening and relentless, and if we are fortunate we can turn being maddening and relentless into a strength. She has taught me that when you have tamed your fear, you harness its power to do extraordinary things. In the end, the only way to save yourself from the grief is to find a way to help others.

Epilogue

The photo Amy Price sent me on August 4, 2014, is still saved on my phone. She could not get her phone to record a video, so instead she sent me a photo of a handsome little boy smiling as he played miniature golf. It was impossible to believe he had the same disease Cal did. I started to think I might faint as I looked at it.

Over the years I have shown it to doctors and priests and social workers. It was my proof of a miracle. It was my hope. I would tell anyone who would listen—friends, colleagues, family members, reporters—"This little boy has Cal's disease. He should be as sick as Cal is, but he isn't; he can play outside." A friend advised me to stop looking at the photo. "You are just torturing yourself," she said. It was hard to explain how much Giovanni's photo did not cause me pain. It saved me. It gave me my purpose. It was my way out of this nightmare of grief and despair.

The photo that Amy sent of her youngest daughter, Cecilia, made me fall out of my chair. At eight months old, Cecilia was a beautiful child with brown eyes, mostly bald save for the wisps of curl. She looked just like my Cal; the resemblance was overwhelming. When, ten days after the doctors told Pat and me that Cal would die, I asked Dr. Waldman to promise me that I would get to meet a little girl with curly hair and brown eyes who would be saved from Cal's fate. But I imagined that would be a long time coming. Today my wish had been granted. It had not taken twenty years. The miracle I had dreamed about happened years ahead of schedule.

Can I tell you what it feels like to behold a miracle? It hurts. It is this electric shock of pain that isn't quite unbearable and doesn't last long. This new pain makes you forget how to get air in your body, and you can't move. You feel as if you are floating away, as though you can't control your muscles. And the miracle's reality is so powerful it takes on a physical form. It is as if you could grab it and pull it close to you.

I had died the moment the doctors told me Cal was dying, and now I had returned from the dead. And as I processed the truth of a miracle, the dull, throbbing pain of watching Cal living every day with this disease ends and gets replaced by this sense that nothing else matters, because I have seen something that was supposed to be impossible. It felt divine, an out-of-body experience; it was as if I was more than myself but not me at all.

Looking at Cecilia's smile and her warm brown eyes, I could see that Cal's suffering *would* change the world and that there was some purpose in it all. This was bigger than me and Cal and my family; it was every child who had come before her and would come after her. I didn't feel the way I used to before Cal was sick, but I was calm and happy, even with the awareness of my grief.

Then I thought of my father, who believed in miracles and was angry when I refused to have faith. A month before he died he told me about a vision of a silent, shimmering woman who would sit by his bedside. He insisted it was Cal coming to see him. He pleaded with me to believe him, not to think it was a hallucination caused by medications or renal failure. I found myself longing to see my father to tell him he had been right about miracles all along.

Cal's life had meaning. Her suffering was not pointless; she had awakened the strength and courage we needed to help other people's children even when she could not be saved. How thrilling it was to experience hope. The fact that the miracle was not Cal's did not cause jealousy or regret. All I experienced was gratitude. These families all had lost one child to the disease; how could anyone begrudge them the chance at a miracle to save the second—and for the Prices, the third?

Helping other people's children will never be enough to make up for losing Cal. My deepest wish still is that I had never heard of leukodystrophy and that my daughter would be running around the house and driving us all crazy. The thing is, until Cal, I didn't understand miracles, and I didn't truly believe in them either.

Here's what I now know: we don't get miracles because we wish for them or pray for them or deserve them—miracles must be earned through sacrifice, hard work, and suffering. Our daughter gave us the gift of witnessing a miracle and, now, the chance to play a minuscule part in creating miracles for others.

Camille is wrapping up her sophomore year at the College of Wooster. At first she did not want to leave home because she worried about being too far from her sister, but we were convinced she should have her own life unencumbered by a home that doubled as a hospital. Camille is majoring in sociology. When she finishes college, she wants to find a way to help care for children like Cal by pursuing some sort of career in medicine. After two summer internships at CHOP, she loves the place; it has become such an important part of our family. But the world may call Camille in a different direction. She wrote a beautiful children's book commissioned by the Pennsylvania Pediatric Palliative Care Coalition titled *Bev and Lil*, and she is working with the illustrator Lela Meunier to finish it. *Bev and Lil* is the story of what it is like to be the sibling of a medically complex child. As far as we know, this is the first book of its kind, and all of us know it will help so many families like ours.

PJ is a high school sophomore who loves basketball, riding his bike (though he is counting the days until he gets a driver's license), music, biology, and computer games. In other words, he is a remarkably and impressively normal young man. He brings dozens of his friends to volunteer at the Cupcake Challenge (which is going into its eighth year and has raised more than $100,000). For many years PJ preferred to be private with his feelings about Cal, but this has changed recently. Much to my and Pat's amazement he agreed to speak to a local reporter about what the cupcakes have meant to him, saying, "It's a great feeling, honestly. Giving other kids a chance that Cal and my family never had is like the best feeling because you really made a difference in their lives." This summer he hopes to get a job at Carlino's market, but he also asked to see if he could intern at the University of Pennsylvania in the lab overseen by Dr. Wilson. He told his father and me, "I want to understand how gene therapy works." When I told him I knew Dr. Erika De Boever, the director of the University of Pennsylvania's Gene Therapy Program, my son was actually impressed.

Pat never complained and managed to work and care for Cal even after two relapses with multiple myeloma. While the doctors had predicted they could keep the cancer at bay for at least a decade, as my father warned me, "the only thing you know about doctor's predictions is that they will be wrong." Pat died on April 16, 2020, surrounded by his children and me right here at home. Pat warned me that he wanted no fuss, no funerals and no priests. And you had to wonder if he had not timed his death around the COVID-19 pandemic to slip out the back door.

Pat would have been so proud of how Camille and PJ were brave and loving during his final weeks. Both children now hover over me like protective hens. Grief has reversed our roles; it seems Camille and PJ are more naturally brave like their father. Cal and I have been less composed about our emotions. I cry all the time, and Cal smiles and laughs less frequently. She and I discussed how Daddy got sick and had to leave us. "He had no choice about this," I tell her, "and wherever he is, he loves you so much." Cal's grief manifests itself in a rage over his absence. One day, the phone rang and suddenly Pat's voice from the answering machine floated through the house. Cal fluttered her eyes open and moved her whole body to locate him. When she realized he would not appear, she fell back to sleep, believing his voice to be a dream.

It was in the last two weeks of his life that Pat allowed me the gift of caring for him. He and I slept in our bed, and with the help of the aides, I fed and dressed him. Years of caring for Cal had prepared me for this. On Easter Sunday, four days before his death, when he held Cal one final time, Cal laughed and sang in his arms, but Pat was weary and pained as he held her. I asked, "What are you thinking, my darling?" And he answered, "I am worried what the future will hold." "But," I said, forcing myself to smile and sound courageous, "you have done everything for us, you have protected us and cared for us. There is nothing left for you to do." I promised, not totally certain I believed the words, "We will be fine." This was the closest thing to comfort and truth I shared with Pat. There would be no dramatic deathbed speeches.

Pat did not leave any letters, or so I thought. But, after he died, and I went through his emails and papers, I discovered spreadsheets with information about the children's education funds and the life insurance carefully organized for me to find. Two months before his death, he had been cashing out of the stock market and moving funds to our checking account so I would not have to worry about money. He had even taken the time to preorder shampoo and diapers for Cal, and Brody's special dog food. He despised that dog most days, but, as he was dying, he took the time to order dog food. What did that say about Pat?

All those times I had longed to talk to him about my feelings and what his death would mean, Pat was in a race against time to take care of us all. On the day I finished this book, Pat declared that he was impressed and a bit jealous that I had finished my fourth book. But, even so, he said he would never read it. He had experienced the events described here once already; he did not want to relive it trapped in my version of reality. But a few days before his death, Pat's younger sister Barbara would send me an essay he had written two months earlier. It was Pat's version of a memoir: about getting his cancer diagnosis and seeing his father, Paddy, for the last time. As he faced death and knew he would be leaving us, he realized that the best way to tame grief is to turn it into a story.

I was struck by the fact that Pat had been inspired by me to be vulnerable and share his story. There was even a line that was an explanation of, and maybe even an apology for, our incompatible styles in the face of grief.

> It was too late, I had already shuttered that part of me off to the rest of the world, and I would deal with my issues in my own way as I had almost always done, without any outside help. I am Irish and repression for us is both unconscious and an art form.

Grief in the time of COVID-19 has brought unique challenges; no friends and family visiting, no wake or proper funeral. But hundreds of mourners organized a drive-by procession on our street, and three hundred people attended a Zoom wake in Pat's honor. It was all beautiful and moving. But what I crave most of all—to collapse into someone's arms weeping, to shake hands and share stories about Pat in our home with music and good beer and food—has been denied to us. Writing this book, and living through the experiences of these last eight years, I have felt like a world-class athlete who has devoted her life to preparing for this defining moment. I had always assumed that Cal would die before Pat, and he would be here to help me. But, since nothing in my life has gone according to plan, it seems Cal, Camille, and PJ are determined to get me through this. Cal has made us all wiser, braver, and more generous than I ever imagined. Cal has helped me take this grief and pain and accomplish things that have served families around the world. And the love and concern from these families have been returned to us many times over this past month. During our time of need, I remain grateful to the incredible community of friends and neighbors and doctors and leukodystrophy families who have our backs and will be there no matter what the future holds. When it is safe to do so, Camille, PJ, and I will be getting tattoos in honor of Pat. Camille has chosen a hen because Pat called her "chicken," and PJ wants a lion because "lions are strong and brave, just like Dad." And I can't decide between the mandolin, which Pat played when he sang to Cal and me, or the Liverpool Football Club motto: "You'll never walk alone."

I have even started running again. To be sure, my running might better be described as aspirational: a more accurate term would be "barely jogging" or a form of fast-walking, where I pump my arms with a determined focus. I am slow, really slow. So slow, in fact, that elderly women with walking sticks lap me. It takes me thirty minutes to do the two-mile circuit.

Grief leads to a trauma-induced depression. And so, the good news is that it appears I can manage the most acute symptoms with the well-documented mood-altering effects of running. After years of trying to run for health and wellness, now I run every day, rain or shine, for survival. People tell me I look tan and more fit than I have in a decade. The compliments roll off. I run to get to my new life. I refuse to get trapped in longing for the past. Mourning Pat is one thing; I will never get over the great love of my life. But aching for our old lives is a waste of time and energy. There is no returning to normal (for any of us). I need to focus on building a new life and finding joy and beauty and purpose in what is possible.

The best thing I can tell you is that I know that, no matter what happens, we will be okay just like I promised Pat.

And the work to cure MLD continues. In October 2019, Pat and I were part of a delegation of MLD families that addressed the Food and Drug Administration. We hope to see Orchard Therapeutics gain FDA approval for a gene therapy to treat Cal's disease. We are confident MLD will join the ranks of the 5 percent of rare diseases with an FDA-approved treatment. This would be one of the first gene therapies in the world to treat an inherited neurological disorder in children. In August 2020, New York State will start screening newborns for MLD. This means we will be able to help kids like Cal in time to save their lives. Passage Bio, the biotech company founded by Jim Wilson, just announced plans to develop a treatment for MLD that it believes might work on children already showing symptoms of the disease. I am heartbroken Pat won't be here to witness these things, but none of it would have been possible without him.

Cal celebrated her tenth birthday on December 23, 2019. We had to return to the hospital on Christmas Eve (as we have had to do on three out of the past five Christmases) because she got pneumonia. During a recent admission, one of the most senior doctors in the pediatric ICU, a nationally recognized expert in the care of children like Cal, admitted amazement at her case: "When I look at your daughter's X-rays, I am perplexed at how they could belong to the child I see lying in the hospital bed." Cal's X-rays suggest a child who should be in acute respiratory distress, needing oxygen and CPAP and maybe even a tracheostomy to stay alive. Yet she still breathes comfortably on room air and no longer has a DNR order in her file.

Cal still has a terminal illness, and she will die too young, but she has exceeded all of our expectations. She sleeps more these days and is more distant, but she laughs and smiles when the people she loves walk into the room and she hears our voices. She is still a bully about the TV and hates sharing the remote with me when I watch *The Rachel Maddow Show*. Cal is a celebrity and her face has appeared on billboards, the front page of the *Philadelphia Inquirer*, the cover of CHOP's magazine, and CBS's *Sunday Morning* with Jane Pauley. Like everyone else, we are terrified about what COVID-19 would mean for Cal. Her doctors have pledged that they won't give up on her if she gets sick. Cal nearly died from a form of the coronavirus back in 2018, and I try not to think about what a hospitalization before a treatment becomes available would mean. So, we are quarantined, terrified even to see her doctors. Sadly, the pandemic has given the general public a taste of what it means to have a medically compromised child, to live in terror of a fever or a cough, and to be forced to isolate yourself from the world to protect the people you love. We never leave the house, but Cal is comfortable and cherished and has, as Father Peter predicted all those years ago, taught all of us the meaning of life.

Acknowledgments

It has taken me six years to write this book. Gayatri Patnaik, my editor at Beacon Press, and my literary agent, Lisa Adams, have shown tremendous patience and faith in me. We were not sure how the story was going to end. We were all surprised by the final product, and I hope it was worth the wait.

Thanks to Dr. Deborah Seagull, who has worked with me since Pat's diagnosis with cancer and has helped me process the emotions and feelings that so often threatened to consume me.

Will Myers helped me transform the raw material in my blogs and essays into a story with chapters and a narrative arc. He is a wonderful and generous editor, and I am so grateful for his advice.

I am indebted to all of the families we work with through Cal's foundation. But special thanks to the Prices, the Scotts, and the Hammonds, whose lives have become inextricably linked to ours.

The brilliant women at the Children's Hospital of Philadelphia (CHOP) come to our rescue on a regular basis: Brenda Banwell, MD; Amy Waldman, MD; Laura Adang, MD, PhD; Adeline Vanderver, MD; Annique Hogan, MD; Erin Prange, RN; Jennifer Hwang, MD; the Pediatric Advanced Care Team (PACT); members of the Leukodystrophy Center at CHOP; Gina Santucci, RN; and Sarah Stoney, MSW.

Our home-based team, who cherish Cal, is led by Margaret "Peggy" Stancavage, Karen Hadley, Renee Gilliam, Michelle Balcer, Amina Deen, and Katie Maratea.

Thanks to my friends Jane Donaldson, Julie MacDonald, Susan Clampet-Lundquist, Jo Parker, Naomi Schneider, and Ashley Fox, who read early drafts of this project and believed there was a *there* there and did not flinch during a series of my nervous breakdowns.

Also to the Schwartzberg family, Spencer and Marissa Golden, Lauren Krivo and Bob Kaufman, Lisa Sonneborn, and Rob and Mary-Ellen Schlaak, who joined us on so many of our cupcake-related (mis)adventures.

I must acknowledge my colleagues at Saint Joseph's University who supported me over the years and provided crucial funding for the completion of this book project during my sabbatical year.

Thanks to our Cynwyd family—most especially Dr. Daniel Martino, Rebecca Brenner, and Maria Wells—at the Cynwyd Elementary School and to the entire Lower Merion School District community, who have transformed me into the "Cupcake Lady" and have sold thousands of cupcakes to help children with leukodystrophy.

Thanks to Father Chris, Michelle Kontos, and our beloved Saint Luke's Greek Orthodox community who have showered our family with so much delicious food, support, and love since they heard Calliope was ill.

Paul Isenberg, of Bringing Hope Home, appeared in my life just when we needed him like a real-life Superman. He was one of my first teachers in the superpower of grief.

Thanks also to Dr. Andrew Shenker and Dr. Erika De Boever, who make me sound more clever than I am.

And I must express my gratitude to my family, most especially my mother, Alice; sisters Nicole and Cathy; brother Robert; children, PJ and Camille; and my late husband, Pat, who have shown tremendous patience with me. The family agreed to do the book only because they understood that it healed me and that all the money raised would go to help other children and families.

Then there is Cal, who has made me believe in miracles, magic, and mermaids.

All the events in the book were written about in my blogs and journals, and all the errors in recounting events are my own.

All the author's royalties will be donated to the Calliope Joy Foundation and a significant portion of the funds will be used to support projects at the Children's Hospital of Philadelphia.

Notes

CHAPTER THREE: MERMAID

1. This would be the second-to-last time Sister Alice and I spoke. When we saw each other in the hallways of the hospital after Cal's physical therapy appointment in November 2012, Sister Alice wanted to talk to me about Cal and our plans to start a foundation to support outreach for terminally ill children. She had handed me her card, embraced me, and promised to talk soon. A month later Sister Alice collapsed and died of a heart attack in the hospital's parking lot. She was caring for patients and their families right until the end and died next door to the emergency room of the Hospital of the University of Pennsylvania, one of the finest in the nation. She was sixty-five. Her loss was mourned by the entire hospital.

2. In the Greek Orthodox faith, married men may be ordained as priests. Their wives are important leaders in the community and are addressed as Presbytera.

CHAPTER SIX: MAKE-A-WISH

1. The Campbell family's story was covered in the Utah media in the series "Our Year with the Campbells"; Aaron and Emily Campbell, "The Campbell Family: A Change in Milestones," *Herald Extra*, February 12, 2014, https://www.heraldextra.com/momclick/parenting/the-campbell-family-a-change-in-milestones/article_768ecd70-4f90-5c9a-a254-4a11ca199e0b.html.

CHAPTER TEN: CUPCAKES

1. In 2009, Patrick Aubourg and his colleagues successfully treated two boys with adrenoleukodystrophy, or ALD. This work marks a high point in the field of gene therapy after years of failure. It was Amber Salzman, a former executive at GlaxoSmithKline, who made

this research possible after her son Spencer and two nephews were diagnosed with ALD. Amber and I would finally meet in 2015 after the launch of the Leukodystrophy Center for Excellence, and she would become a dear friend and colleague in this work. In a remarkable coincidence, Amber and her family live just a few blocks from us in suburban Philadelphia. Not enough people are aware of Amber's pivotal role in the gene therapy renaissance through her foundation Stop ALD, but her story has been chronicled in Ricki Lewis's book *The Forever Fix.* You can also read Gina Kolata's October 5, 2017, *New York Times* article "In a First, Gene Therapy Halts a Fatal Brain Disease," https://www.nytimes.com/2017/10/05/health/gene-therapy-brain-disease.html.

CHAPTER ELEVEN: INVESTING IN MIRACLES

1. Carl June, transcript of TEDMED lecture, "A 'Living Drug' That Could Change the Way We Treat Cancer," November 12, 2018, https://www.ted.com/talks/carl_june_a_living_drug_that_could_change_the_way_we_treat_cancer/transcript?language=en.

2. June, "A 'Living Drug.'"

3. June, "A 'Living Drug.'"

4. June, "A 'Living Drug.'"

5. June, "A 'Living Drug.'"

6. The first time I heard the term "Cellicon Valley" was during the Life Sciences Pennsylvania Meeting in 2016. Since then the term has gained more traction, but here is just one of the articles that describes Philadelphia this way: "I can make the argument that Philadelphia has the greatest concentration of foundational research in gene and cell therapy in the world," says Spark CEO Jeffrey Marrazzo, whose company made history with the first FDA treatment approved for a genetic disorder in 2017. Don Steinberg, "Welcome to Cellicon Valley?" *Philadelphia* magazine, June 17, 2017, https://www.phillymag.com/business/2017/06/17/cellacon-valley-philadelphia-medical-technology.

7. Each year, just over four million babies are born in the United States. Virtually all of them have a heel pricked to draw a few drops of blood that is then analyzed to check for a number of serious, yet treatable, disorders. What makes this program so essential is that babies with these conditions usually look completely healthy at birth, so tests are needed to uncover hidden diseases. This straightforward testing tells whether a baby needs immediate intervention to treat a disorder that otherwise would have gone undetected until the disease progressed to the point of disability—or death.

8. In 2006, New York, partly because of Jim Kelly's efforts, became the first state in the nation to screen for Krabbe diseases. In 2014, Pennsylvania lawmakers passed "Hannah's Law," which added Krabbe disease and five other disorders to the Pennsylvania newborn screening list. Sponsored by State Representative Angel Cruz of Philadelphia, the bill was inspired by the struggles of Hannah Ginion, who was diagnosed with Krabbe disease, the same disease that Hunter Kelly had.